INTRODUCTION

This revision guide is matched to the AQA Modular specifications for Separate Sciences. In other words it covers the six additional modules which together with the modules in Double Award Science form a suite of 18 modules representing the three separate sciences.

In this guide, the first three modules are those that are tested by modular test, namely: MOVING AND FEEDING; AQUEOUS AND ORGANIC CHEMISTRY and PHYSICS IN ACTION. The remaining three modules in the guide are those which are tested in the terminal examination, namely: BIOLOGY IN ACTION; CHEMISTRY IN ACTION and FORCES AND MOTION. The two differing methods of assessment are reflected in the summary questions at the end of each module.

Everything the student needs to know is contained within this slim volume, but in addition, to make things even easier, we've condensed each module down to a single page of last minute 'Key Points' for that final recap before the exam.

A great deal of care has been taken in the production of this revision guide and many phone calls have been made to AQA to clarify the meaning of sections of the specification. As a result, some parts of the specification are amplified or reduced accordingly.

It is also worth mentioning here that material in the first three modules which may be tested again in the terminal examination is outlined by red boxes. Similarly, throughout this volume, material which is HIGHER TIER only is indicated by the presence of a pale blue background.

This guide is intended as a source of first rate revision material for GCSE students but it is also our hope that it eases the burden of over worked Science Departments.

Mary James

Mary James – **Editor**

The Tested Modules

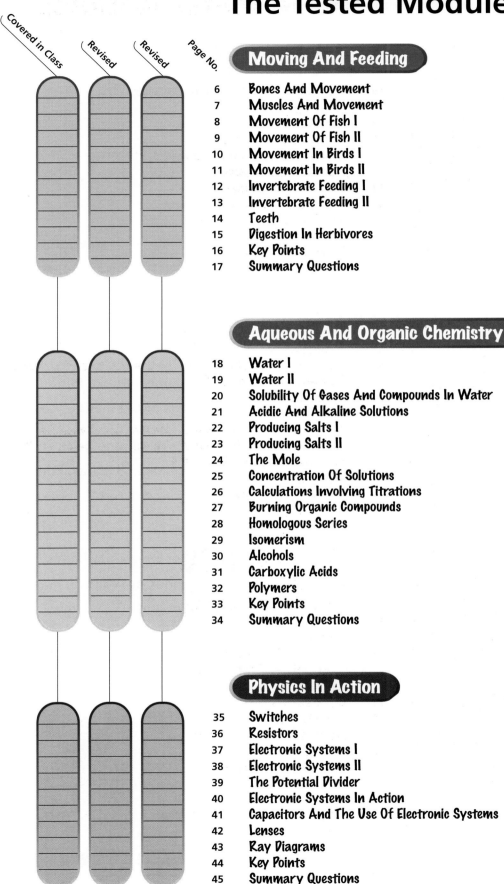

The Terminal Modules

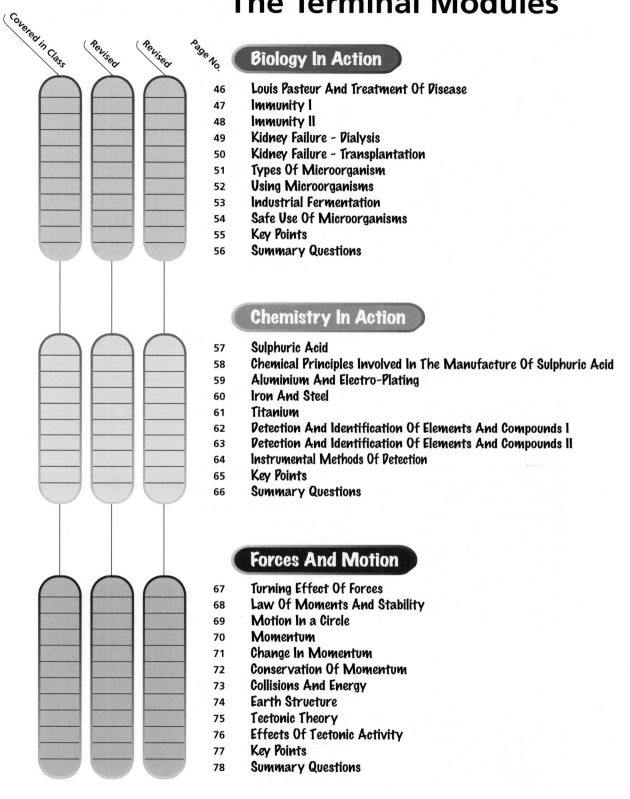

Covered in Class   Revised   Revised   Page No.

HOW TO USE THIS REVISION GUIDE

- In certain places we have included slightly more than the specification suggests you need to know. For instance in FORCES AND MOTION we use the equation for kinetic energy to calculate energy before and after a collision even though the equation isn't in the specification. This is as a result of talking with AQA and researching past papers. In some cases we have expanded on a point - purely to aid understanding. Other than this we have adhered to the principle that the guide should contain 'everything you need to know, and nothing else', in a highly refined, user-friendly format.

- Don't just read the guide! LEARN ACTIVELY! Constantly test yourself WITHOUT LOOKING AT THE TEXT.

- When you have revised a small sub-section or diagram, PLACE A BOLD TICK AGAINST IT, and also tick the 'Covered In Class' and 'Revised' sections of the Contents page as you progress. This is great for your self-confidence.

- Jot down anything that you think will help you to remember - no matter how trivial it may seem.

> For your Terminal Examination remember to revise the areas outlined in red boxes in the first three modules of this guide. These, like the red boxes in the year 10 guide ('Tested Modules') can be tested again in your Terminal Examination.

Any sections of this guide which are intended for HIGHER TIER candidates only are indicated by the presence of a pale blue background. Check with your teacher as to whether you should revise these.

SOME IMPORTANT FACTS ABOUT THE ASSESSMENT OF THESE MODULES

- The first three modules in this guide are assessed by MODULAR TESTS. These consist of ten objective questions (multiple choice) of different types which can be taken at various specified dates throughout year 10 or year 11.

- The remaining three modules in this guide ie. BIOLOGY IN ACTION; CHEMISTRY IN ACTION and FORCES AND MOTION are assessed by written examination consisting of compulsory structured questions including extended writing. There will be a one and a half hour paper for each of BIOLOGY, CHEMISTRY and PHYSICS, consisting of the following:

BIOLOGY	CHEMISTRY	PHYSICS
• INHERITANCE AND SELECTION	• STRUCTURES AND BONDING	• WAVES AND RADIATION
• ENVIRONMENT	• PATTERNS OF CHEMICAL CHANGE	• FORCES
• BIOLOGY IN ACTION	• CHEMISTRY IN ACTION	• FORCES AND MOTION
plus aspects of ...	plus aspects of ...	plus aspects of ...
*Humans As Organisms	*Metals	*Energy
*Maintenance Of Life	*Earth Materials	*Electricity
**Moving And Feeding	**Aqueous And Organic Chemistry	**Physics In Action

*The bits that will be tested from these modules are OUTLINED IN RED in VOLUME I of Science: Double Award Modular (The Tested Modules).

** The bits to be tested from these modules are OUTLINED IN RED in this guide.

Internal Skeleton

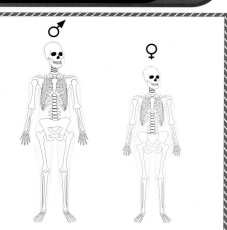

Vertebrates have an INTERNAL SKELETON which provides the framework for SUPPORT and MOVEMENT.

• SUPPORT is provided by the rigidity of the skeleton which also holds the organs in place and provides a protective casing for some of the vital organs eg. brain, heart and lungs.

• MOVEMENT is achieved due to the fact that many of the larger bones in the body are held together by freely moveable joints. This enables us to bend our bodies and move our limbs quite extensively by contracting our muscles. Muscles only move bones by contraction.

Joints

A joint, as the name implies, is a connection between two bones. In some cases there may be very little movement allowed eg. the bones of the skull and pelvis. However other joints may display an extensive range of movement eg. the shoulder and hip joints.

Joints are brilliantly adapted to perform their function ...

The Hip Joint

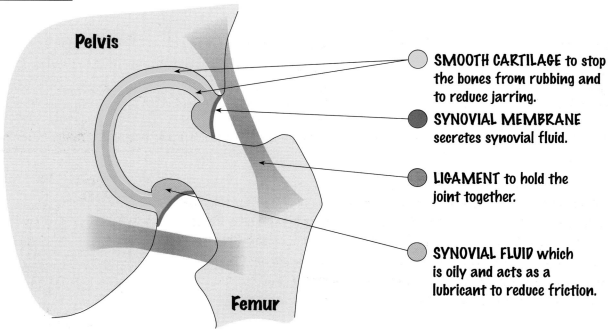

Pelvis

Femur

SMOOTH CARTILAGE to stop the bones from rubbing and to reduce jarring.

SYNOVIAL MEMBRANE secretes synovial fluid.

LIGAMENT to hold the joint together.

SYNOVIAL FLUID which is oily and acts as a lubricant to reduce friction.

Adaptation To Function Of Skeletal Tissues

Skeletal tissues have physical properties which make them well adapted to perform their various functions ...

BONE: resists compression, bending and stretching because it is hardened by deposits of calcium phosphate. However living bone cells and protein fibres prevent it from being brittle.

CARTILAGE: covers the ends of bones in joints and is strong and resilient, but NOT rigid! This enables it to be compressed slightly so that it can act as a shock absorber. This reduces jarring between the ends of moving bones.

LIGAMENTS: attach bones to other bones. They have high tensile strength (resist stretching forces) but are elastic enough to allow joints to bend without fear of dislocation.

TENDONS: attach muscles to bones and also have high tensile strength. However they have very little elasticity in order to transfer the maximum amount of muscle movement to the bone which is to be moved (see next page).

Muscle Attachment

Muscles are attached to your skeleton by TENDONS, usually across a synovial joint. These tendons are fibrous.

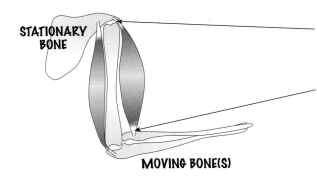

STATIONARY BONE

MOVING BONE(S)

At one end of the muscle, a tendon joins the muscle to the fixed or stationary bone.

At the other end of the muscle, a tendon joins the muscle to the bone that it moves.

As muscles contract they shorten and movement occurs.

How Muscles Work

Muscles can only create movement by becoming shorter and so at least two muscles are needed around a joint (you may remember ANTAGONISTIC MUSCLES from Key Stage 3).

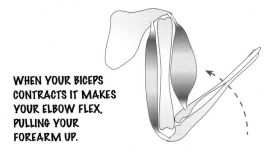

WHEN YOUR BICEPS CONTRACTS IT MAKES YOUR ELBOW FLEX, PULLING YOUR FOREARM UP.

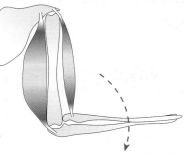

TO ALLOW YOUR ELBOW TO EXTEND, YOU NEED YOUR TRICEPS TO CONTRACT AND PULL YOUR ARM BACK DOWN. (OR RELY ON GRAVITY!)

Joints such as the shoulder joint have more muscle attachments to provide an even greater range of movement.

Energy Needs Of Muscle Tissue

The muscle tissue we use to move our skeleton is made up of individual muscle fibres consisting of individual cells which have fused together. These fibres form bundles which join together to form specific muscles. These fibres use energy from RESPIRATION to contract. Consequently, the harder they work, the more glucose and oxygen they need to produce energy, and the more carbon dioxide and heat they produce.

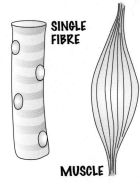

SINGLE FIBRE

MUSCLE

GLUCOSE OXYGEN → WORKING MUSCLE → CARBON DIOXIDE HEAT

Increased heart rate causes the blood to flow more quickly through the muscle tissue to provide OXYGEN and GLUCOSE and to remove CARBON DIOXIDE and HEAT.

The Benefits Of Regular Exercise

Regular exercise keeps muscles toned (slightly tensed and ready to contract), increases muscle strength (without stiffness and soreness after exercise), keeps joints working smoothly and promotes a healthy circulation to the muscles, the heart and the lungs. HOWEVER, care should be taken to avoid sprains (the tearing of ligaments and other tissues in a joint) and to avoid dislocations (when a bone is forced out of a joint).

SPRAINS

DISLOCATIONS

+

MUSCLE TONE

MUSCLE STRENGTH

HEALTHY JOINTS

GOOD CIRCULATION

Adaptations For Moving In Water

An adaptation is a biological solution to an environmental challenge. When we say that fish are well adapted to their environment we mean that they have characteristics which make them well suited to survive in an aquatic environment. These characteristics are shaped by the process of evolution. The following three examples show how fish are adapted for movement in a watery medium.

Streamlined Shape

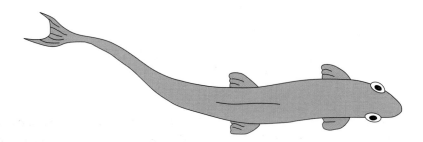

Fish have a streamlined body shape to reduce the force due to the resistance of the water as the fish cuts through it. Although there is a huge range of variation in the size and shape of fish, this principle still holds true. Even in fish with huge bulbous heads, the 'tear drop' shape can still be seen.

Wave-like Body Movement

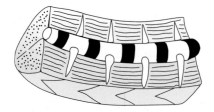

The diagram above shows the vertebra and muscles in the mid-section of a fish. You will notice how the muscles are arranged in zig-zag shaped blocks (these are particularly easy to see in cooked salmon). These muscles on each side of the vertebral column alternately contract and relax to produce a wave-like motion along the length of the body. This provides propulsion, but more importantly causes powerful movements of the tail fin.

Tail Fin With A Large Surface Area

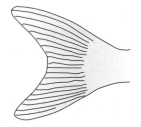 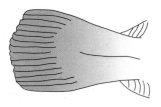 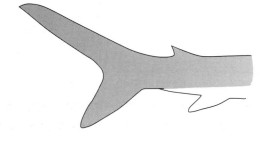

Tail fins come in all shapes and sizes (and colours), but basically their main function is to provide a large surface area with which to push backwards against the water. The wave-like movement caused by the muscles in the body is therefore transferred to a thrusting force to push the fish forwards.

Controlling Movement In Water

Fish need to exercise control over their position in the water, to remain in a relatively upright position, and to control changes of direction. The following structures help the fish to achieve these aims.

The Swim Bladder

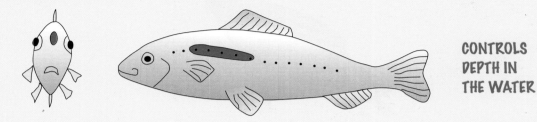

CONTROLS DEPTH IN THE WATER

The swim bladder is an internal organ found in bony fish (ie. not sharks and rays). Its function is to provide buoyancy, but the degree of buoyancy can be regulated by either adding or removing gas. The more gas the bladder contains, the more buoyant the fish will be and the higher it will rise in the water. Removing gas causes the fish to sink lower in the water.

The Median Fins

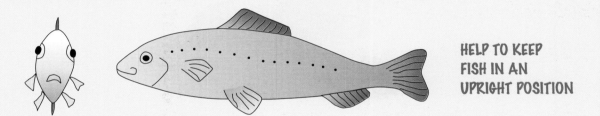

HELP TO KEEP FISH IN AN UPRIGHT POSITION

There are usually one or more of the following median fins: a DORSAL fin (on the back of the fish), a VENTRAL fin (on the belly of the fish) and the tail fin. These are all in the same plane and run along the mid line of the fish. Consequently they increase the vertical surface area, and therefore tend to keep the fish in an upright position.

The Paired Fins

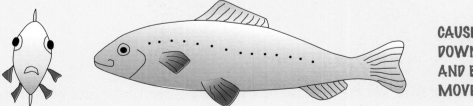

CAUSE UPWARDS, DOWNWARDS AND BACKWARDS MOVEMENT

There are usually two sets of these paired fins. One pair is situated towards the front end of the fish while the other is situated slightly further back. Unlike the median fins which are largely static, the paired fins are capable of a good range of movement. They can be angled so that thrust from the tail can take the fish on an upwards or downwards course, or they can fan forwards or backwards to achieve finer movements when the fish is at rest.

Adaptations For Moving In Air

The evolution of flight is perhaps one of the most remarkable examples of evolution in the whole of nature. Most birds are adapted for flight and as such show characteristics which enable them to excel in an aerial environment. Examples of these are shown below.

Streamlined Body Shape

Birds have a streamlined body shape to reduce the force of drag due to the resistance of the air as the bird flies along. This aerodynamic shape is helped by the design of the wings but both the shape of the bird's body and its covering of feathers help to reduce drag.

Large Surface Area Of Wings

The wings of birds provide a large surface area compared to the body of the bird. This enables them to push downwards more effectively on the air and therefore provide lift. The wings of soaring and gliding birds such as the albatross and the vulture provide an enormous area for energy-efficient flight.

Arrangement Of Flight Feathers

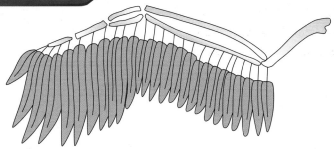

Feathers are a key feature of birds, and the flight feathers in the wings provide the large wing area. They manage to combine great structural strength with incredible lightness in an arrangement which provides the most lift.

Honeycomb Bones

The bones in the wing are riddled with air spaces which reduce the mass of the bone without a significant reduction in strength. This feature makes it possible for birds to have such relatively large wing areas.

Further Adaptations For Moving In Air

In addition to the features mentioned on the previous page Higher Tier candidates are expected to know these four slightly more sophisticated examples of adaptations for flight.

Aerofoil Wing Shape

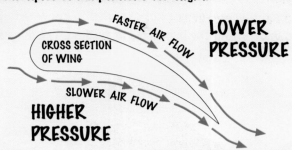

Wings act as aerofoils due to their shape. The shape ensures that air flows more quickly over their upper surfaces than their lower surfaces, resulting in lower pressure above the wing and higher pressure beneath it. This generates lift and therefore assists flight.

Interlocking Barbs Of The Flight Feathers

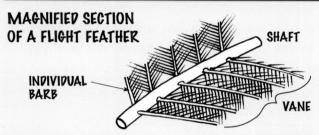

Each feather consists of a vane made up of individual barbs. These barbs have hooked branches which interlock with the branches of the two adjacent barbs to provide a flat surface for flight. In addition to this the flight feathers have a hollow shaft to reduce weight.

Arrangement Of Primary And Secondary Flight Feathers

The arrangement of the primaries (yellow opposite) and secondaries (green opposite) enable the downbeat of the wings to provide both lift and forward propulsion. On the upstroke the feathers part slightly to allow airflow between them. This reduces air resistance and therefore less energy is required during the wing's recovery stroke.

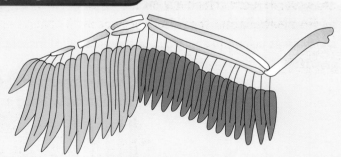

Features Of The Skeleton

- The large sternum (breastbone) and keel give a large surface area and a rigid framework for muscle attachment. Particularly for the huge muscles needed in flight.

- The arrangement of the bones in the wing has evolved from the typical pentadactyl (five fingered) limb also found in humans. Birds however have less digits and wrist bones compared to the human limb.

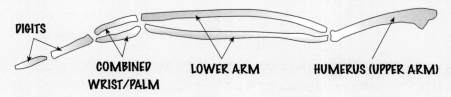

Feeding In Mussels

Mussels belong to a group of animals called molluscs. This group includes animals as diverse as slugs, snails, squids and octopuses. Mussels are FILTER FEEDERS. In other words they filter microscopic organisms called plankton out of the water. This is their food source. You are not expected to know details of the internal structure of a mussel but you are expected to understand the principles of feeding. The diagram summarises them for you:

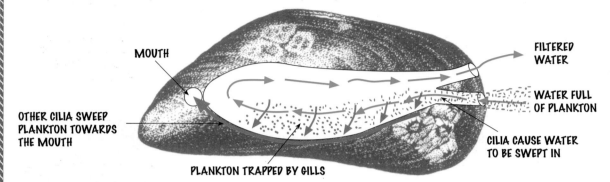

MOUTH

FILTERED WATER

WATER FULL OF PLANKTON

OTHER CILIA SWEEP PLANKTON TOWARDS THE MOUTH

CILIA CAUSE WATER TO BE SWEPT IN

PLANKTON TRAPPED BY GILLS

1. Hair-like cilia beat to draw a current of water across the gills which remove oxygen but also filter out plankton by acting as a sort of sieve.
2. This water is then expelled from the mussel and now contains much less oxygen and very little plankton.
3. The plankton which has been filtered out of the water by the gills is now swept towards the mouth by another set of cilia where it enters the digestive system.

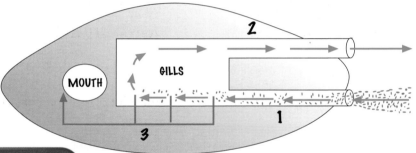

MOUTH

GILLS

2

1

3

Feeding In Mosquitoes

Mosquitoes belong to the group of animals called insects. They feed on blood and in order to do so they must first penetrate the skin of their victim.

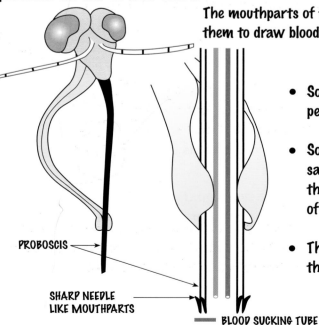

The mouthparts of the mosquito show several ingenious adaptations to help them to draw blood successfully ...

- Some mouthparts form sharp needle-like lances which can penetrate skin easily. These form part of the proboscis.

- Some mouthparts form tubes. One of these transports saliva down into the blood. The saliva contains a substance that prevents the blood from clotting. These also form part of the proboscis.

- There are special muscles in the throat that help to draw the blood from the penetrated capillary.

PROBOSCIS

SHARP NEEDLE LIKE MOUTHPARTS

BLOOD SUCKING TUBE
SALIVA TUBE

Mosquitoes And The Malarial Parasite

Parasites are organisms that live in or on another organism and obtain food from it.
The saliva of the mosquito may contain a parasite which causes MALARIA. This malarial parasite is a single-celled organism which feeds and reproduces inside human red blood cells.

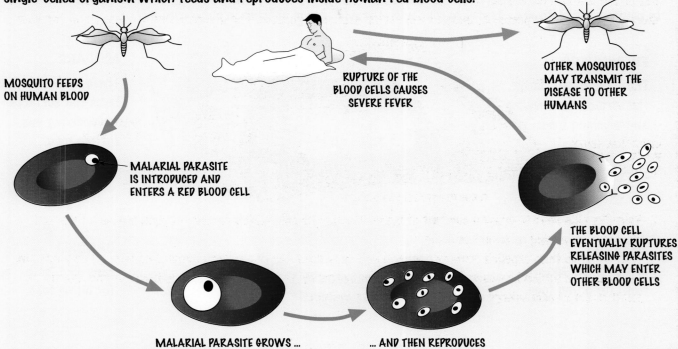

MOSQUITO FEEDS
ON HUMAN BLOOD

RUPTURE OF THE
BLOOD CELLS CAUSES
SEVERE FEVER

OTHER MOSQUITOES
MAY TRANSMIT THE
DISEASE TO OTHER
HUMANS

MALARIAL PARASITE
IS INTRODUCED AND
ENTERS A RED BLOOD CELL

THE BLOOD CELL
EVENTUALLY RUPTURES
RELEASING PARASITES
WHICH MAY ENTER
OTHER BLOOD CELLS

MALARIAL PARASITE GROWS ...

... AND THEN REPRODUCES

Feeding Adaptations In Other Insects

Aphids (eg. greenfly), butterflies and houseflies also feed by sucking fluids into their mouths.

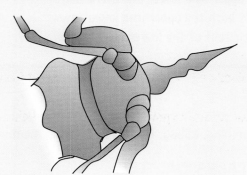

APHIDS feed on phloem sap and have very fine stylets which they push into the phloem. The phloem is under pressure and so is pushed through the stylet and into the aphid's digestive system.

BUTTERFLIES feed on nectar which is produced deep down in the flower. To reach it, they have a long-coiled proboscis (like a hose pipe) which can be moved around like an elephant's trunk. When it's not in use it's kept coiled up beneath the insect's head.

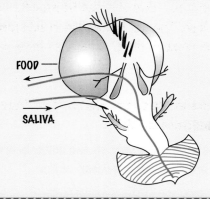

FOOD

SALIVA

HOUSEFLIES can change solid food into liquid food by secreting saliva onto it. This then predigests the food externally turning it into a mushy liquid. The liquid only is then sucked up into the fly's body.

Teeth For A Varied Diet

Mammals have teeth which may be used to bite off pieces of food and to chew it into smaller pieces before swallowing. The shapes of teeth are suited to their function.

In humans the teeth are adapted to cope with the wide range of foods in our varied diet.

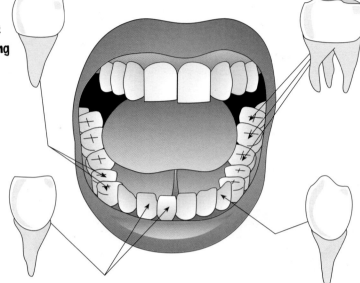

PREMOLARS
These teeth have large flat surfaces for chewing and crushing food.

MOLARS
These teeth also have large flat surfaces for chewing and cutting food.

INCISORS
Sharp, chisel-edged teeth for biting food.

CANINES
Fang-like teeth for biting food.

Dentition

This word describes the number and arrangement of teeth in an animal. The human mouth above has 2 incisors; 1 canine; 2 premolars and 3 molars on each side of both the upper and lower jaws. The dog's mouth shown below has 3 incisors; 1 canine; 4 premolars on each side of both the upper and lower jaws, but there are 2 molars on one half of the upper jaw and 3 molars on one half of the lower jaw.

Teeth For A Carnivorous Diet

Dogs have teeth and jaws that are adapted for a carnivorous diet, ie. catching, killing, tearing and eating meat.

CANINES
These are longer, sharper and more pointed and may be used to grip prey or to tear meat.

CARNASSIAL TEETH
These are formed from the last premolar of the upper jaw and the first molar of the lower jaw. They are large teeth with sharp edges which are used to sheer meat and crush bones.

INCISORS
These are small and can be used to pull meat from bones.

JAWS
The jaws move only up and down in order to provide a firm scissor-action.

Digestion Of Cellulose

The digestive systems of mammals are adapted to their diet. Mammals do not produce enzymes which are capable of breaking down cellulose, the substance which forms the walls of plant cells. This means that herbivorous mammals have to rely on cellulose-digesting bacteria which live in specific places in their digestive systems. These bacteria enable them to break down cellulose to sugars.

The relationship between cellulose-digesting bacteria and herbivores is an example of MUTUALISM. This means that both organisms benefit from the relationship in the sense that the herbivores obtain sugar from cellulose and the bacteria are provided with cellulose and other nutrients.

Naturally enough carnivorous mammals don't harbour these bacteria.

Digestion In Sheep And Cows

Sheep and cows have a RUMEN between the oesophagus and stomach which contains these bacteria.

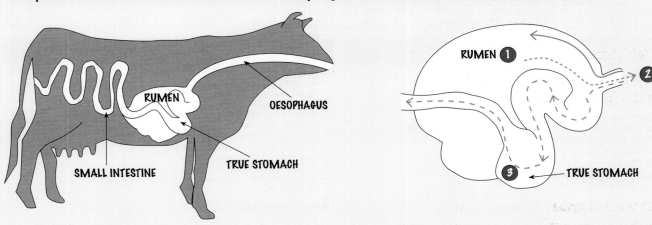

1 Grass is first cropped and then swallowed directly into the rumen where the cellulose-digesting enzymes start to break down the cellulose into sugars.

2 Eventually, the contents of the rumen are regurgitated in small amounts to be 're-chewed' in the mouth ('chewing the cud'). This enhances the digestion of the already part-digested contents of the rumen.

3 After this the material passes to the true stomach before travelling through the small intestine.

Digestion In Rabbits

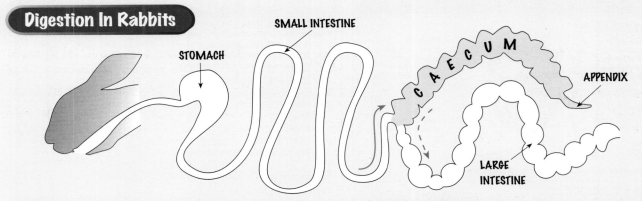

Rabbits have their cellulose-digesting bacteria in a large CAECUM/APPENDIX which opens into the junction between the small and large intestines. Once the bacteria have done their work, the material passes down the large intestine and leaves via the anus. This material is rich in nutrients including sugars and so the rabbit eats these faeces to extract the nutrients via its small intestine. This time the waste material passes straight through and is not re-eaten.

BONES, MUSCLES AND MOVEMENT

INTERNAL SKELETON: provides the framework for SUPPORT and MOVEMENT.

JOINTS:

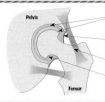

- **SMOOTH CARTILAGE** to stop the bones from rubbing and to reduce jarring.
- **SYNOVIAL MEMBRANE** secretes synovial fluid.
- **LIGAMENT** to hold the joint together.
- **SYNOVIAL FLUID** which is oily and acts as a lubricant to reduce friction.

ADAPTATION TO FUNCTION OF SKELETAL TISSUE:
BONE resists compression, bending and stretching due to deposits of calcium phosphate.
CARTILAGE acts as a shock absorber. LIGAMENTS attach bones to bones.
TENDONS attach muscles to bones.

ENERGY NEEDS OF MUSCLE TISSUE: Muscle tissue consists of fibres which contract when supplied with energy from respiration.
Harder work results in faster transport of materials to and from the cell.

BENEFITS OF EXERCISE: MUSCLE TONE, MUSCLE STRENGTH, HEALTHY JOINTS, GOOD CIRCULATION. AVOID SPRAINS AND DISLOCATIONS.

MOVEMENT OF FISH

ADAPTATIONS FOR MOVING IN WATER:
1. STREAMLINED SHAPE: reduces water resistance
2. WAVE-LIKE BODY MOVEMENT: produced by zig-zag muscle blocks.
3. TAIL FIN WITH LARGE SURFACE AREA: provides backward thrusting force.

CONTROLLING MOVEMENT IN WATER:
1. The SWIM BLADDER: controls depth in the water.
2. The MEDIAN FINS: keep the fish upright by increasing the vertical surface area.
3. The PAIRED FINS: enable up, down and backwards movement. There are usually two sets of these.

MOVEMENT IN BIRDS

ADAPTATIONS FOR MOVING IN AIR:
1. STREAMLINED BODY SHAPE reduces air resistance.
2. LARGE SURFACE AREA OF WINGS to push down on the air to provide lift.
3. ARRANGEMENT OF FLIGHT FEATHERS combine structural strength with lightness.
4. HONEYCOMB BONES reduce mass but retain strength.
5. AEROFOIL WING SHAPE generates lift due to pressure differences.
6. INTERLOCKING BARBS OF THE FLIGHT FEATHERS, provide a flat surface for flight.
7. ARRANGEMENT OF PRIMARY AND SECONDARY FLIGHT FEATHERS enables the downbeat to produce lift and forward propulsion but allows airflow on upbeat.
8. LARGE STERNUM AND KEEL provide area for muscle attachment.
   - Bird limbs have evolved from the typical PENTADACTYL LIMB.

INVERTEBRATE FEEDING

FEEDING IN MUSSELS
- Cilia draw a current of water across the gills which filter out plankton.
- The plankton which has been filtered out is swept toward the mouth by another set of cilia.

FEEDING IN MOSQUITOES
- Some mouthparts form needle-like proboscis.
- Some form tubes, one of which transports saliva and a substance to prevent clotting.
- Special muscles in the throat draw blood up another tube.

FEEDING ADAPTATIONS IN OTHER INSECTS
- APHIDS feed on phloem sap which flows into them under pressure.
- BUTTERFLIES feed on nectar which they reach via their long, coiled proboscis.
- HOUSEFLIES secrete saliva onto food which predigests it into a mush which they suck up.

THE MALARIAL PARASITE

MOSQUITO FEEDS ON HUMAN BLOOD

MALARIAL PARASITE IS INTRODUCED AND ENTERS A RED BLOOD CELL

MALARIAL PARASITE GROWS ...

... AND THEN REPRODUCES

RUPTURE OF THE BLOOD CELLS CAUSES SEVERE FEVER

THE BLOOD CELL EVENTUALLY RUPTURES RELEASING PARASITES WHICH MAY ENTER OTHER BLOOD CELLS

OTHER MOSQUITOES MAY TRANSMIT THE DISEASE TO OTHER HUMANS

TEETH

TEETH FOR A VARIED DIET

PREMOLARS
These teeth have large flat surfaces for chewing and crushing food.

MOLARS
These teeth also have large flat surfaces for chewing and cutting food.

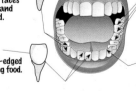

INCISORS
Sharp, chisel-edged teeth for biting food.

CANINES
Fang-like teeth for biting food.

DENTITION
This describes the number and arrangement of the teeth.

Above this would be 2 incisors : 1 canine : 2 premolars : 3 molars

TEETH FOR A CARNIVOROUS DIET

CANINES
These are longer, sharper and more pointed and may be used to grip prey or to tear meat.

INCISORS
These are small and can be used to pull meat apart.

CARNASSIAL TEETH
These are formed from the last premolar of the upper jaw and the first molar of the lower jaw. They are large teeth with sharp edges which are used to sheer meat and crush bones.

JAWS
The jaws move only up and down in order to provide a firm scissor-action.

DIGESTION IN HERBIVORES

DIGESTION OF CELLULOSE
Mammals don't produce an enzyme to break down cellulose. Herbivorous mammals often have cellulose-digesting bacteria in their digestive system which break down cellulose to sugars. This relationship is an example of mutualism, since both organisms benefit from the relationship. Carnivorous mammals don't have these bacteria.

DIGESTION IN SHEEP AND COWS
1. Grass enters the rumen where cellulose-digesting enzymes start to break down cellulose to sugars.
2. The contents of the rumen are regurgitated and chewed again.
3. The food then passes to the true stomach.

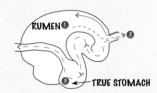

RUMEN ❶   ❷

❸   TRUE STOMACH

DIGESTION IN RABBITS

Rabbits have cellulose-digesting bacteria in a large caecum/appendix. Once the bacteria have done their work the material passes through the large intestine. It is still rich in nutrients, including sugars, and therefore rabbits eat their own faeces so that these can be absorbed in the small intestine before being finally excreted.

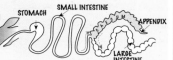

STOMACH   SMALL INTESTINE   APPENDIX   LARGE INTESTINE

1. The table below is about skeletal tissues. Match words from the list with each of the numbers 1-4 in the table.

   A. BONE.
   B. CARTILAGE.
   C. LIGAMENTS.
   D. TENDONS

   1. Attach bones to other bones but are elastic enough to allow movement.
   2. Resists bending, compression and stretching due to deposits of calcium phosphate.
   3. Attach muscles to bones but have very little elasticity to ensure maximum movement.
   4. Covers the ends of bones to reduce friction and jarring.

2. The sentences below are about the control of movement in fish. Match words from the list with each of the spaces 1-4 in the sentences.

   A. ZIG ZAG MUSCLE BLOCKS.
   B. WATER RESISTANCE.
   C. STREAMLINED SHAPE.
   D. TAIL FIN.

   The ___1___ of fish allows them to cut through water easily by reducing ___2___. The force is produced by movements of the ___3___ which is powered by the contraction of ___4___ in the body of the fish.

3. Fins are found on most fish. Which TWO of the following statements are correct about fins?
   A. The median fins control the depth of the fish in the water.
   B. The paired fins keep the fish upright in the water.
   C. The median fins keep the fish upright in the water.
   D. The tail fin controls the depth of the fish in the water.
   E. The paired fins enable up, down and backwards movements.

4. Regular exercise contributes to good health.
4.1 Which one of the following is NOT a benefit of regular exercise?
   A. Increased muscle tone.
   B. Increased strength.
   C. Increased intelligence.
   D. Better circulation.

4.2 The skeleton provides the framework for ...
   A. NERVOUS CONTROL AND MOVEMENT.
   B. SUPPORT AND MOVEMENT.
   C. SUPPORT AND NERVOUS CONTROL.
   D. NERVOUS CONTROL AND CIRCULATION.

4.3 Muscle fibres need energy to contract. They get this energy from ...
   A. Muscle fibres need energy to contract. They get this energy from ...
   A. PHOTOSYNTHESIS.
   B. EXTENSION.
   C. OXYGEN.
   D. RESPIRATION.

4.4 Contracting muscle fibres produce, as waste products, ...
   A. CARBON DIOXIDE AND OXYGEN.
   B. CARBON DIOXIDE AND GLUCOSE.
   C. CARBON DIOXIDE AND HEAT.
   D. CARBON DIOXIDE AND MOVEMENT.

5. Birds are well designed, or adapted, for movement through air.
5.1 The streamlined body shape of birds ...
   A. REDUCES AIR RESISTANCE.
   B. REPELS WATER.
   C. INCREASES LIFT.
   D. REDUCES WEIGHT.

5.2 The overall weight of birds is reduced by ...
   A. EATING LESS
   B. POWERFUL FLIGHT MUSCLES.
   C. AIR SPACES IN THE BONES.
   D. FLUFFING OUT THE FEATHERS.

5.3 Flight is assisted by the aerofoil wing shape which causes ...
   A. LOWER PRESSURE ABOVE THE WING THAN BENEATH IT.
   B. HIGHER PRESSURE ABOVE THE WING THAN BENEATH IT.
   C. EQUAL PRESSURES ABOVE AND BELOW THE WING.
   D. ZERO PRESSURE ABOVE THE WING.

5.4 The arrangement of the primary and secondary flight feathers allows ...
   A. the recovery stroke to provide lift and forward propulsion.
   B. air to flow between them on the recovery stroke.
   C. air to flow between them on the downbeat of the wings.
   D. a completely airtight surface for flight.

6. Feeding in vertebrates and invertebrates shows many different adaptations.
6.1 Which one of the following is NOT an adaptation for feeding in mosquitoes?
   A. Some mouthparts form sharp needle-like lances.
   B. Special muscles in the throat help to draw blood from the victim.
   C. Some mouthparts form tubes which transport saliva and blood.
   D. Some mouthparts are adapted to cut through flesh.

6.2 Which one of the following is an adaptation for feeding in butterflies?
   A. Very fine stylets for removing phloem under pressure.
   B. A long, coiled proboscis for feeding on nectar
   C. The ability to predigest food by secreting saliva over it
   D. Needle-like mouthparts for deep penetration of tissues.

6.3 The jaws of mammals often contain teeth with sharp, chisel edges which are used for biting food into smaller more manageable pieces. These are called ...
   A. MOLARS.
   B. PREMOLARS.
   C. CANINES.
   D. INCISORS.

6.4 Carnivorous mammals have teeth with sharp edges in the upper and lower jaw which can sheer meat from the bone and can even crush bones! These are called ...
   A. MOLARS.
   B. PREMOLARS.
   C. CARNASSIALS.
   D. INCISORS.

7. Herbivores have a digestive system which is adapted to their diet.
7.1 Herbivorous mammals break down cellulose by ...
   A. PRODUCING CELLULASE ENZYMES.
   B. RELYING ON CELLULOSE DIGESTING BACTERIA.
   C. RECYCLING THEIR FAECES.
   D. CHEWING PLANT MATERIAL FOR LONG PERIODS.

7.2 Mutualism means ...
   A. A relationship where both organisms benefit.
   B. A relationship where neither organism benefits.
   C. A relationship where one organism benefits.
   D. A relationship where both organisms are disadvantaged.

7.3 In sheep and cows, the cellulose-digesting bacteria are contained in the ...
   A. SMALL INTESTINE.
   B. LARGE INTESTINE.
   C. TRUE STOMACH.
   D. RUMEN.

7.4 In rabbits, the cellulose-digesting bacteria are contained in the ...
   A. CAECUM/APPENDIX.
   B. LARGE INTESTINE.
   C. SMALL INTESTINE.
   D. STOMACH.

The Water Cycle

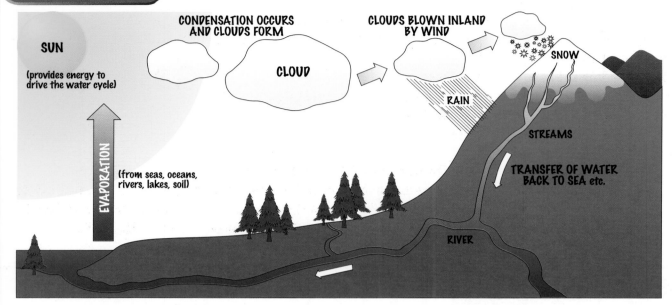

- Energy from the **SUN** causes water in rivers, lakes and oceans to rise via **EVAPORATION**.
- As the water vapour rises higher and higher into the atmosphere it cools and condensation occurs ...
- ... forming droplets of water which collect together to form **CLOUDS**.
- As the clouds rise further they cool and rain is produced when the droplets are big enough ...
- ... and the whole cycle begins again.

The Importance Of Water

Water is the most abundant substance on the surface of the Earth and it is essential for the existence of all life. It is an important raw material and has many uses. These include its use ...

 ... as a **SOLVENT** where substances are dissolved in it.

 ... as a **COOLANT** for the removal of heat from a system.

 ... in many industrial processes including the manufacture of **SULPHURIC ACID**.

Drinking Water

There are **TWO** main steps in producing water which is safe to drink ...

(1) The water is passed through a **FILTER BED** to remove any solid particles.

(2) **CHLORINE** gas is then added to kill any harmful bacteria.

Contamination Of Water

Farmers use artificial fertilisers to replace the nitrogen in the soil used up by previous crops - so that crop yields can be maintained. To be effective, fertilisers must be soluble in water. The use of too much fertiliser results in dissolved **NITRATE** and **AMMONIUM IONS** being 'washed out' of the soil into natural waters such as rivers and lakes. The level of dissolved nitrate ions in water must be carefully monitored as they can indirectly reduce the ability of haemoglobin to carry oxygen. Babies are most at risk and the effect is known as 'blue baby' syndrome.

Soft And Hard Water

Tap water can usually be described as being 'soft' or 'hard'. Soft water readily forms a lather with soap. Hard water however contains dissolved compounds which react with soap to form SCUM, making it less easy to form a lather.

The DISADVANTAGES of hard water are...

• ... MORE SOAP is needed to form a lather which increases costs ...

• ... it often leads to DEPOSITS called SCALE forming in HEATING SYSTEMS and KETTLES. This reduces their efficiency.

The ADVANTAGES of hard water are ...

• ... the dissolved compounds in it are good for your HEALTH such as calcium compounds that help in the development of STRONG BONES and TEETH. They also help to reduce the development of HEART ILLNESSES.

Formation Of Hard Water

Water is a solvent and many compounds can dissolve in it. Some of these compounds make the water 'hard'. Most hard water contains CALCIUM or MAGNESIUM COMPOUNDS which dissolve in natural water that flows over ground or rocks containing compounds of these elements.

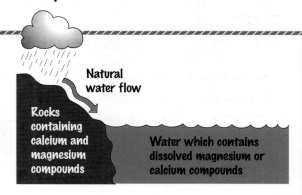

Natural water flow

Rocks containing calcium and magnesium compounds

Water which contains dissolved magnesium or calcium compounds

Removing Hardness

To make hard water soft, all we have to do is remove the dissolved CALCIUM and MAGNESIUM IONS contained in it. To do this we can ...

1 ... ADD SODIUM CARBONATE SOLUTION, which is washing soda, to it. The CARBONATE IONS react with the CALCIUM and MAGNESIUM IONS to form CALCIUM CARBONATE and MAGNESIUM CARBONATE respectively which precipitate out of solution as they are both insoluble. For example, ...

CALCIUM SULPHATE + SODIUM CARBONATE $\longrightarrow$ SODIUM SULPHATE + CALCIUM CARBONATE

$CaSO_{4(aq)}$ + $Na_2CO_{3(aq)}$ $\longrightarrow$ $Na_2SO_{4(aq)}$ + $CaCO_{3(s)}$
(washing soda) (precipitate)

2 ... pass the hard water through an ION-EXCHANGE COLUMN.

HARD WATER IN (contains Ca^{2+}/Mg^{2+} ions)

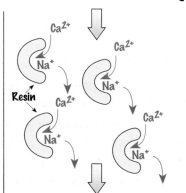

The column contains a special RESIN which provides a plentiful supply of HYDROGEN IONS, $H^+_{(aq)}$ or SODIUM IONS, $Na^+_{(aq)}$. As the hard water passes through the resin, the calcium and magnesium ions contained in it are replaced by hydrogen or sodium ions from the resin. The calcium and magnesium ions consequently remain in the resin.

The resin has to be replaced when it 'runs out' of hydrogen or sodium ions.

SOFT WATER OUT (contains no/very few Ca^{2+}/Mg^{2+} ions)

Solubility Of Gases

Many gases are soluble in water. The SOLUBILITY of these gases INCREASES ...
• ... as the TEMPERATURE of the water DECREASES or ...
• ... as the PRESSURE on the water INCREASES.
Three gases that are soluble are ...

1. CARBON DIOXIDE
Dissolving carbon dioxide under high pressure produces CARBONATED WATER, which is used in fizzy drinks such as lemonade. Releasing the pressure (by unscrewing the bottle top) results in carbon dioxide bubbling out of the solution. Also, keeping drinks in the fridge increases the solubility of CO_2 and keeps them fizzy.

2. OXYGEN
Oxygen dissolves in water and this dissolved oxygen is essential for aquatic life. However, the discharge of hot water from power stations reduces the amount of oxygen dissolved in the water. This lack of oxygen can damage aquatic life.

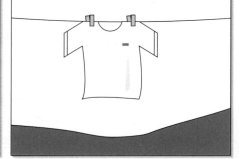

3. CHLORINE
Dissolving chlorine gas in water produces CHLORINE WATER. Chlorine water can be used to bleach materials ie. remove any colour and also it can be used to kill bacteria.

Solubility Of Compounds

In general ...
• ... MOST IONIC COMPOUNDS eg. sodium chloride, copper sulphate are SOLUBLE in water.
• ... MOST COVALENT COMPOUNDS eg. silicon dioxide are INSOLUBLE in water.

The solubility of a solute in water (or another solvent) is usually given in GRAMS OF SOLUTE PER 100 GRAMS OF WATER ie. g/100g AT THAT TEMPERATURE. The temperature of the solvent plays an important part and the solubility of most solutes increases as the temperature increases. This can be shown using a SOLUBILITY CURVE. Below is a typical solubility curve for copper sulphate in water.

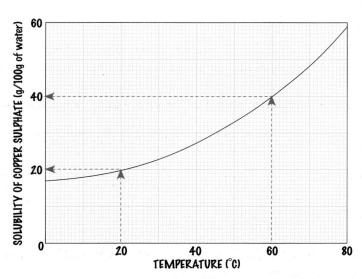

1 Any point on the curve tells us the maximum amount of copper sulphate that dissolves at a particular water temperature to give us a SATURATED SOLUTION.
eg. at 20°C it is 20g/100g of water
eg. at 60°C it is 40g/100g of water

2 When a warm saturated solution of copper sulphate cools down some of the copper sulphate will separate from the solution and CRYSTALLISATION occurs eg. if the solution is cooled down from 60°C to 20°C then 40g - 20g = 20g of copper sulphate per 100g of water will crystallise out.

Acids And Alkalis

Some compounds react with water to produce ACIDIC or ALKALINE solutions.

On their own these compounds do not exhibit any acidic or alkaline characteristics. Water must be present for a substance to act as an acid or as a base.

- All ACIDS, in aqueous solution, dissociate to produce H^+ ions.

  eg. If we take hydrochloric acid ...

The H^+ ion is simply a PROTON and in water this proton is hydrated (ie. chemically bonded to water) and is represented as $H^+_{(aq)}$. It is the presence of the $H^+_{(aq)}$ ions that gives the solution its acidic characteristics.

- All ALKALIS, however, in aqueous solution, dissociate to produce OH^- ions.

  eg. if we take sodium hydroxide ...

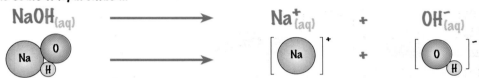

This time the presence of the $OH^-_{(aq)}$ ions gives the solution its alkaline characteristics.

Arrhenius, Lowry And Brönsted

The idea that aqueous solutions of acids contain $H^+_{(aq)}$ ions was first introduced by the Swedish chemist Svante Arrhenius in 1887. He put forward the theory that some substances spontaneously dissociate into ions when they dissolve in water. At the time this idea was quite revolutionary and it took a long time for it to be accepted since chemists realised that a H^+ ion is just a proton and that such a small particle cannot exist on its own.

However, in 1923 the Danish chemist Johannes Brönsted and the English chemist T.M. Lowry both proposed separately a new theory of acids and bases. This theory had many advantages over the one previously put forward by Arrhenius.

Brönsted put forward the idea that ...

... an ACID can be defined as a PROTON DONOR and ...

... a BASE can be defined as a PROTON ACCEPTOR.

However an acid cannot donate a proton unless there is an appropriate base available to accept it.

Strength Of Acids And Alkalis

Acids and alkalis are classified by the extent of their ionisation in water.

- A STRONG ACID or ALKALI is one that is 100% ionised in water ie. all the compound dissociates into ions. Examples of strong acids are HYDROCHLORIC, SULPHURIC and NITRIC ACIDS while examples of strong alkalis are SODIUM and POTASSIUM HYDROXIDE.
- A WEAK ACID or ALKALI, however, is one that is only partially ionised in water ie. not all of the compound dissociates into ions.

Examples of weak acids are ETHANOIC, CITRIC and CARBONIC ACIDS while an example of a weak alkali is AMMONIA SOLUTION.

You should also be aware that you can have different acids of the same concentration which have different pH values. It simply depends on the extent of their ionisation in water. Strong acids will therefore register a much lower pH than weak acids on the pH scale.

Acids can also be distinguished by their rate of reaction with METALS to produce 'metal salts' and hydrogen. Strong acids will react more vigorously with the metal compared to a weak acid.

SALTS can be produced by several methods. You will need to be familiar with the practical details of salt preparation, although there are variations within each method. Here are **FIVE** typical ways of producing them.

1. Reaction Of A Metal With An Acid

eg. MAGNESIUM + SULPHURIC ACID $\longrightarrow$ MAGNESIUM SULPHATE + HYDROGEN

$$Mg_{(s)} + H_2SO_{4(aq)} \longrightarrow MgSO_{4(aq)} + H_{2(g)}$$

Magnesium is added in excess to the sulphuric acid until no more hydrogen gas is produced. The reaction is complete.

Filter to remove any magnesium that has not reacted. The beaker now contains a saturated solution of the salt, magnesium sulphate.

Filter to separate the crystals from any solution left behind. The crystals are then removed, washed and left to dry.

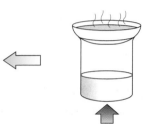

Evaporate slowly until crystals form on the end of a cold glass rod placed in the solution. Leave to cool and crystallise.

2. Reaction Of An Insoluble Base With An Acid

Bases are the **OXIDES** and **HYDROXIDES** of metals

eg. COPPER OXIDE + SULPHURIC ACID $\longrightarrow$ COPPER SULPHATE + WATER

$$CuO_{(s)} + H_2SO_{4(aq)} \longrightarrow CuSO_{4\ (aq)} + H_2O_{(l)}$$

Excess copper oxide is added to the sulphuric acid until no more will dissolve and the reaction is complete. After that the practical procedure follows that of the second stage above in order to obtain crystals of the salt.

NB THE ABOVE METHODS WILL ONLY WORK FOR SOLUBLE SALTS.

3. Reaction Of A Soluble Base With An Acid

A soluble base is called an **ALKALI**. Acids react with alkalis to produce a salt and water. The reaction is known as **NEUTRALISATION**.

eg. HYDROCHLORIC ACID + SODIUM HYDROXIDE $\longrightarrow$ SODIUM CHLORIDE + WATER

$$HCl_{(aq)} + NaOH_{(aq)} \longrightarrow NaCl_{(aq)} + H_2O_{(l)}$$

- Add the hydrochloric acid to the sodium hydroxide gradually, in small amounts, stirring constantly.
- After each addition of acid use a glass rod to remove a drop of the solution and test using indicator paper whether the solution has become neutral.
- Repeat with further additions of acid until a neutral solution is obtained. The reaction is now complete.

The salt, sodium chloride, can now be retrieved from the solution by evaporation using the same practical procedures as above.

4. Mixing Two Solutions To Form An Insoluble Salt (Precipitation)

The two salts in 1 and 2 are both formed in aqueous solution and the salt is obtained by crystalisation.
Sometimes the salt formed is insoluble and is called a **PRECIPITATE**.

eg. BARIUM CHLORIDE + SODIUM SULPHATE $\longrightarrow$ BARIUM SULPHATE + SODIUM CHLORIDE

$$BaCl_{2(aq)} \quad + \quad Na_2SO_{4(aq)} \quad \longrightarrow \quad BaSO_{4(s)} \quad + \quad NaCl_{(aq)}$$

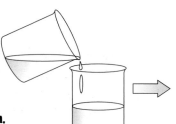

Sodium sulphate solution is added to barium chloride solution. A white precipitate of barium sulphate and aqueous sodium chloride is produced in the. reaction.

Filter the mixture to leave behind solid barium sulphate. The barium sulphate is then washed to remove any excess sodium chloride and left to dry.

5. Direct Combination Of The Elements To Form Anhydrous Salts

eg.   IRON   +   CHLORINE $\longrightarrow$ IRON (III) CHLORIDE

$$2Fe_{(s)} \quad + \quad 3Cl_{2(g)} \quad \longrightarrow \quad 2FeCl_{3(s)}$$

Iron, in the form of iron wool, is heated strongly while **CHLORINE** gas is passed over it in a fume cupboard. The iron wool will glow brightly as it reacts with the chlorine to produce anhydrous (without water) iron (III) chloride.

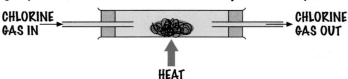

CHLORINE GAS IN — CHLORINE GAS OUT

HEAT

Another example is the reaction of aluminium with chlorine gas ...

ALUMINIUM   +   CHLORINE $\longrightarrow$ ALUMINIUM CHLORIDE

$$2Al_{(s)} \quad + \quad 3Cl_{2(g)} \quad \longrightarrow \quad 2AlCl_{3(s)}$$

Titration

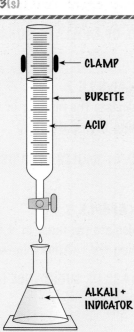

TITRATION is an accurate technique which can be used to find out how much of an acid is needed to neutralise an alkali.

- A **PIPETTE** which has been carefully washed and rinsed with the alkali is used to measure out a known and accurate volume of the alkali, using a pipette filler.
  The alkali is placed in a clean and dry **CONICAL FLASK**.
  A suitable indicator is added. (eg. phenolphthalein)

- Acid is placed in a **BURETTE** which has been carefully washed and rinsed with the acid. An initial reading of the volume of acid in the burette is taken.
  The acid is carefully added to the alkali until the indicator changes colour to show neutrality. This is called the end-point. A final reading is taken of the volume of acid in the burette. You will now be able to calculate the volume of acid added.

  This can then be repeated to check results and can then be done without an indicator if we want to obtain the salt.

CLAMP
BURETTE
ACID
ALKALI + INDICATOR

The Mole

- A MOLE (mol) is a measure of the number of 'particles' contained in a substance. One mole of any substance (element or compound) will always contain the same number of particles (atoms or molecules). (Six hundred thousand billion billion or 6×10^{23}!)
- The MASS OF ONE MOLE OF A SUBSTANCE called the MOLAR MASS (g/mol) is always equal to the RELATIVE ATOMIC MASS, A_r of the substance in grams, if the substance is an ELEMENT, ...

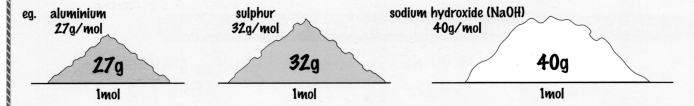

A_r of hydrogen atom	A_r of carbon atom	A_r of oxygen atom	A_r of sodium atom	A_r of magnesium atom	A_r of sulphur atom	A_r of potassium atom
1	12	16	23	24	32	39

... or the RELATIVE FORMULA MASS, M_r (A_rs of all its elements added together) of the SUBSTANCE in GRAMS, if the substance is a COMPOUND.

eg.　aluminium
27g/mol

27g

1mol

sulphur
32g/mol

32g

1mol

sodium hydroxide (NaOH)
40g/mol

40g

1mol

Questions involving moles can be calculated using the following relationship.
However, THIS RELATIONSHIP WILL NOT BE GIVEN TO YOU IN THE EXAMINATION.

$$\text{NUMBER OF MOLES OF SUBSTANCE (mol)} = \frac{\text{MASS OF SUBSTANCE (g)}}{\text{MASS OF ONE MOLE (g/mol)}}$$

EXAMPLE 1
Calculate the number of moles of carbon in 36g of the element.
Using the relationship ...

$$\text{NO. OF MOLES OF SUBSTANCE (mol)} = \frac{\text{MASS OF SUBSTANCE (g)}}{\text{MASS OF ONE MOLE (g/mol)}} = \frac{36g}{12g/mol} = 3mol$$

EXAMPLE 2
Calculate the number of moles of carbon dioxide in 33g of the gas.
Using the relationship ...

$$\text{NO. OF MOLES OF SUBSTANCE (mol)} = \frac{\text{MASS OF SUBSTANCE (g)}}{\text{MASS OF ONE MOLE (g/mol)}} = \frac{33g}{44g/mol} = 0.75mol$$

EXAMPLE 3
Calculate the mass of 4 moles of sodium hydroxide.
Using the relationship, which is rearranged ...

MASS OF SUBSTANCE (g) = NO. OF MOLES OF SUBSTANCE (mol) x MASS OF ONE MOLE (g/mol)
= 4mol x 40g/mol = 160g

These calculations can be done using RATIOS depending on the level of the student's mathematical ability.

The CONCENTRATION of an aqueous solution is usually expressed by stating how many MOLES of a particular solute are present in each CUBIC DECIMETRE of solution. Concentration is measured in moles per cubic decimetre (mol dm^{-3} or M). One cubic decimetre is the same as 1000cm^3 or 1 litre.
If we take a solution that has a concentration of ...

... 1mol dm^{-3}

 ... then 1mol of solute is present in every 1dm^3 of solution

... 0.5mol dm^{-3}

 ... then 0.5mol of solute is present in every 1dm^3 of solution

... 2mol dm^{-3}

 ... then 2mol of solute is present in every 1dm^3 of solution

Questions involving concentration of solutions can be calculated using the following relationship.
Again, **THIS RELATIONSHIP WILL NOT BE GIVEN TO YOU IN THE EXAMINATION.**

$$\text{CONCENTRATION OF SOLUTION (mol dm}^{-3}\text{ or M)} = \frac{\text{NUMBER OF MOLES OF SOLUTE (mol)}}{\text{VOLUME OF SOLUTION (dm}^3)}$$

EXAMPLE 1

Calculate the concentration of an aqueous solution if 2mol of solute is present in 0.5dm^3 of solution.
Using the relationship ...

$$\text{CONC}^N \text{ OF SOLUTION (mol dm}^{-3}) = \frac{\text{NUMBER OF MOLES OF SOLUTE (mol)}}{\text{VOLUME OF SOLUTION (dm}^3)}$$

$$= \frac{2\text{mol}}{0.5\text{dm}^3} = 4\text{mol dm}^{-3}$$

EXAMPLE 2

Calculate the concentration of an aqueous solution if 96g of sodium hydroxide is present in 1500cm^3 of water.
We need the amount of NaOH in MOLES and volume of water in dm^3.

96g of NaOH $= \frac{96}{40} = 2.4$mol (see previous page) and 1500cm^3 of water $= \frac{1500}{1000} = 1.5$dm^3

Using the relationship ...

$$\text{CONC}^N \text{ OF SOLUTION (mol dm}^{-3}) = \frac{\text{NUMBER OF MOLES OF SOLUTE (mol)}}{\text{VOLUME OF SOLUTION (dm}^3)}$$

$$= \frac{2.4\text{mol}}{1.5\text{dm}^3} = 1.6\text{mol dm}^{-3}$$

EXAMPLE 3

An aqueous solution of potassium hydroxide has a volume of 0.5dm^3 and concentration of 0.25mol dm^{-3}.
Calculate the number of moles and mass of KOH present in the solution.
Using the relationship, which is rearranged ...

NUMBER OF MOLES OF SOLUTE (mol) = CONC^N OF SOLUTION (mol dm^{-3}) x VOLUME OF SOLUTION (dm^3)
$$= 0.25\text{mol dm}^3 \text{ x } 0.5\text{dm}^3$$
$$= 0.125\text{mol}$$

To calculate mass of KOH present in the solution we need to use the relationship from the previous page ...

MASS OF SUBSTANCE (g) = No. OF MOLES OF SUBSTANCE (mol) x MASS OF ONE MOLE (g/mol)
$$= 0.125\text{mol x } 56\text{g/mol}$$
$$= 7\text{g}$$

> Alternatively, these calculations can be done using RATIOS depending on the level of the student's mathematical ability.

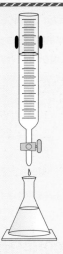

TITRATION can be used to find the CONCENTRATION of an ACID or ALKALI providing we know ...
- ... the relative VOLUMES of acid and alkali used.
- ... the CONCENTRATION of either the acid or the alkali.

You will need to break down the calculation into three stages.

STAGE 1
From the given balanced equation you will be able to determine the ratio of number of moles of acid to alkali for the reaction taking place.

STAGE 2
Calculate the number of moles in the solution of known volume and concentration.
You will now know the number of moles in the other solution from stage 1.

STAGE 3
Calculate the concentration of the other solution.

One important point
You will need to use the relationship from the previous page at stages 2 and 3.

EXAMPLE 1
A titration is carried out and $0.04dm^3$ of hydrochloric acid neutralises $0.08dm^3$ of sodium hydroxide of concentration $1mol\ dm^{-3}$. Calculate the concentration of the hydrochloric acid.

STAGE 1

$$HCl_{(aq)} \quad + \quad NaOH_{(aq)} \longrightarrow NaCl_{(aq)} \quad + \quad H_2O_{(l)}$$

As you can see 1 mole of HCl neutralises <u>1 mole</u> of NaOH.

STAGE 2
NUMBER OF MOLES OF NaOH (mol) = $CONC^N$ of NaOH $(mol\ dm^{-3})$ x VOLUME OF NaOH (dm^3)
$$= 1mol\ dm^{-3} \times 0.08dm^3 = 0.08mol$$

NUMBER OF MOLES OF HCl USED UP IN THE REACTION IS ALSO 0.08mol

STAGE 3
$$CONC^N\ OF\ HCl\ (mol\ dm^{-3}) = \frac{NUMBER\ OF\ MOLES\ OF\ HCl\ (mol)}{VOLUME\ OF\ HCl\ (dm^3)} = \frac{0.08mol}{0.04dm^3} = 2mol\ dm^{-3}$$

EXAMPLE 2
A titration is carried out and $0.035dm^3$ of sulphuric acid of concentration $0.6mol\ dm^{-3}$ neutralises $0.14dm^3$ of sodium hydroxide. Calculate the concentration of the sodium hydroxide.

STAGE 1

$$H_2SO_{4(aq)} \quad + \quad 2NaOH_{(aq)} \longrightarrow Na_2SO_{4(aq)} \quad + \quad 2H_2O_{(l)}$$

This time 1 mole of H_2SO_4 neutralises <u>2 moles</u> OF NaOH.

STAGE 2
NUMBER OF MOLES OF H_2SO_4 (mol) = $CONC^N$ OF H_2SO_4 $(mol\ dm^{-3})$ x VOLUME OF H_2SO_4 (dm^3)
$$= 0.6mol\ dm^{-3} \times 0.035dm^3 = 0.021mol$$

NUMBER OF MOLES OF NaOH USED UP IN THE REACTION IS 2 x 0.021 = 0.042mol

STAGE 3
$$CONC^N\ OF\ NaOH\ (mol\ dm^{-3}) = \frac{NUMBER\ OF\ MOLES\ OF\ NaOH\ (mol)}{VOLUME\ OF\ NaOH\ (dm^3)} = \frac{0.042mol}{0.14dm^3} = 0.3mol\ dm^{-3}$$

Alternatively, these calculations can be done using RATIOS depending on the level of the student's mathematical ability.

COAL, CRUDE OIL, NATURAL GAS and WOOD all contain ORGANIC COMPOUNDS. An organic compound is simply a substance that contains CARBON. Some organic compounds are used as fuels. When a fuel burns it reacts with oxygen from the air. The addition of oxygen to a substance is known as OXIDATION.

Complete Combustion

When organic compounds are burned in a plentiful supply of air then COMPLETE COMBUSTION occurs.
The CARBON is oxidised to CARBON DIOXIDE ...

... and the HYDROGEN is oxidised to WATER.
If we take the complete combustion of methane, CH_4 ...

$$\text{METHANE} + \text{OXYGEN} \longrightarrow \text{CARBON DIOXIDE} + \text{WATER}$$
$$CH_{4(g)} + O_{2(g)} \longrightarrow CO_{2(g)} + 2H_2O_{(l)}$$

Incomplete Combustion

Sometimes the organic compound burns without sufficient oxygen eg. in a room with poor ventilation. Then INCOMPLETE COMBUSTION takes place and instead of carbon dioxide being produced, CARBON MONOXIDE is formed ...

$$\text{METHANE} + \text{OXYGEN} \longrightarrow \text{CARBON MONOXIDE} + \text{WATER}$$
$$2CH_{4(g)} + 3O_{2(g)} \longrightarrow 2CO_{(g)} + 4H_2O_{(l)}$$

Carbon monoxide is a toxic, colourless and odourless gas which combines irreversibly with the haemoglobin in red blood cells reducing the oxygen-carrying capacity of the blood. This would result in death through a lack of oxygen reaching body tissues.

However if there is very little oxygen available, CARBON is produced instead ...

$$\text{METHANE} + \text{OXYGEN} \longrightarrow \text{CARBON} + \text{WATER}$$
$$CH_{4(g)} + O_{2(g)} \longrightarrow C_{(s)} + 2H_2O_{(l)}$$

Overall Evaluation Of The Different Fossil Fuels

Choosing a fuel to use for a particular job requires a careful study of available data. You may well be asked to evaluate the cost, efficiency and cleanliness of burning different fossil fuels using this data. For instance ...

METHANE, CH_4, is a colourless gas. It is non-toxic but is a greenhouse gas.
It is readily available through normal gas supplies. 1 gram of methane produces 55.6kJ of energy when completely burnt.

BUTANE, C_4H_{10}, is used as camping gas. It is easier to store and carry about. It burns in the same way as methane but only 26.9kJ of energy is produced from 1 gram when it burns.

COAL is readily available, not very expensive and releases quite a lot of energy when burnt. The main problem is POLLUTION and in particular the sulphur dioxide (acid rain) gas it produces along with smoke and other pollutants.

Burning Plastics And Other Organic Compounds

Burning plastics and other organic compounds not only produces gases that pollute the air but also fumes that are poisonous especially when there is a limited supply of air.

- If it contains CHLORINE then HYDROGEN CHLORIDE gas is produced. This is a choking, poisonous gas with the formula $HCl_{(g)}$. If it contains NITROGEN then HYDROGEN CYANIDE gas is produced. This is a very poisonous gas with the formula $HCN_{(g)}$.

Also ...

... the combustion products of CARBON and HYDROGEN are formed.

A HOMOLOGOUS SERIES is a family of compounds ...
... which have a GENERAL FORMULA ...
... and have SIMILAR CHEMICAL PROPERTIES.

The Alkanes

The SATURATED HYDROCARBONS form a homologous series called ALKANES ...
... with a general formula C_nH_{2n+2} where n = 1 (for the simplest alkane) 2 ,3, 4 and so on.

Name of alkane	METHANE	ETHANE	PROPANE	BUTANE
n	1	2	3	4
Chemical Formula	CH_4	C_2H_6	C_3H_8	C_4H_{10}
Structure				

You will notice that the hydrocarbons above all contain single bonds only. For this reason they are said to be saturated.

The Alkenes

The UNSATURATED HYDROCARBONS form a homologous series called ALKENES ...
... with a general formula C_nH_{2n} where n = 2 (for the simplest alkene), 3, 4, 5 and so on.

Name of alkene	ETHENE	PROPENE	BUTENE	PENTENE
n	2	3	4	5
Chemical Formula	C_2H_4	C_3H_6	C_4H_8	C_5H_{10}
Structure				

This time you will notice that each hydrocarbon contains a carbon $=$ carbon double bond. For this reason they are said to be unsaturated and it is impossible to have n=1 in the series above.

Reactions Of Alkanes and Alkenes

Both alkanes and alkenes undergo COMBUSTION reactions. However the alkenes are more reactive than alkanes because of the presence of the carbon $=$ carbon double bond. Because of this double bond the alkenes also undergo ADDITION REACTIONS in which one of the carbon $=$ carbon double bonds breaks allowing each carbon atom to form a COVALENT BOND with another atom. For example ...

❶ An alkene will react with hydrogen in the presence of a catalyst to form an alkane.

❷ An alkene will react with bromine water which it decolourises.

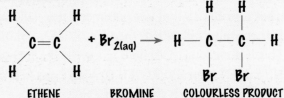

Also ...
VEGETABLE OILS which contain unsaturated fats are liquid. To harden them HYDROGEN is added on to some of the carbon carbon double bonds. The final product is known as MARGARINE.

Isomers

BUTANE, C_4H_{10}, has TWO isomers ...

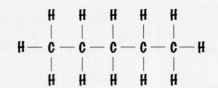

... while PENTANE, C_5H_{12}, has THREE isomers ...

Isomerism occurs when two or more compounds have the SAME CHEMICAL FORMULA ...
... but DIFFERENT STRUCTURES.

Properties Of Isomers

Isomers have DIFFERENT PHYSICAL PROPERTIES which depend upon the strength of the INTERMOLECULAR FORCES of attraction between neighbouring isomers. If we take three isomers (and there are many more) for octane, C_8H_{18} ...

 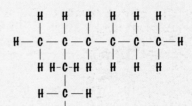

The strength of the intermolecular forces ...

1 ... INCREASES as the carbon chain length increases. This increases the area 'in contact' with neighbouring isomers which results in longer chain isomers having HIGHER BOILING POINTS.

2 ... DECREASES as the amount of chain branching increases. This decreases the area 'in contact' and they don't pack as well which results in these isomers having LOWER BOILING POINTS.

Predicting The Structures Of Isomers

You will need to be able to predict some of the structures of the isomers of given higher alkanes.
Here are some tips.

- Always start with the easiest isomer by drawing one long chain of carbon atoms.
- You can then branch off one of the carbon atoms from your chain to give you your second isomer. You can then repeat by branching off another carbon atom and so on.

But remember ...

- Every carbon atom must have FOUR COVALENT BONDS.
- Every hydrogen atom has ONE COVALENT BOND.

And finally ...

- Check the total number of carbon and hydrogen atoms you have in your isomer. They must add up to the number of carbon and hydrogen atoms in the formula!

Ethanol

ETHANOL, or alcohol as it is better known in everyday life, is one member of a family of substances called ALCOHOLS. Ethanol can be used as ...

... a SOLVENT   ... a FUEL   ... a component in ALCOHOLIC DRINKS

NO AIR IN → ↑ CARBON DIOXIDE OUT

Production Of Ethanol

❶ Ethanol can be produced by the FERMENTATION of SUGARS. WATER and YEAST are mixed with the raw materials at just above room temperature. ENZYMES which are biological catalysts found in the yeast react with the sugars to form ETHANOL and CARBON DIOXIDE.

The carbon dioxide is allowed to escape the reaction vessel ...

... but AIR is prevented from entering it.

The ethanol is separated from the reaction mixture by FRACTIONAL DISTILLATION when the reaction is over.

WATER + YEAST + SUGARS

One problem with the production of ethanol is that it can be OXIDISED by air in the right conditions to produce ETHANOIC ACID. The presence of ethanoic acid results in alcoholic drinks turning sour.

❷ Ethanol can also be produced by reacting STEAM with ETHENE at a MODERATELY HIGH TEMPERATURE and PRESSURE in the presence of the catalyst, phosphoric acid.

$$\text{ETHENE + STEAM} \xrightarrow{\text{phosphoric acid}} \text{ETHANOL}$$

To evaluate the two methods of ethanol production, a number of factors have to be considered.

These are shown in the table opposite ...

... small quantities are best made by method 1.

... large quantities are best made by method 2.

FACTOR	METHOD 1 (FERMENTATION)	METHOD 2 (ETHENE + STEAM)
RATE	SLOW	FAST
QUALITY	FAIRLY GOOD, AFTER FRACTIONAL DISTILLATION	GOOD
BATCH OR CONTINUOUS	BATCH	CONTINUOUS
USE OF RESOURCES	RENEWABLE	NON-RENEWABLE

Alcohols And Their Reactions

The two simplest alcohols are ...

... METHANOL: ... ETHANOL: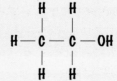

Alcohols form a HOMOLOGOUS SERIES with the functional group — OH. The presence of the — OH gives alcohols their characteristic properties.

Alcohols react ...

❶ ... REVERSIBLY with CARBOXYLIC ACIDS to form ESTERS and WATER.

    eg. ETHANOL + ETHANOIC ACID ⇌ ETHYL ETHANOATE + WATER

(Carboxylic acids and esters are dealt with in more detail on the next page).

❷ ... with SODIUM to form HYDROGEN.

And finally ...

CHOLESTEROL which is a steroid contains the alcohol group — OH. It is an essential steroid to humans.

However ...

the production of too much cholesterol can cause HEART DISEASE.

Carboxylic Acids

These form a HOMOLOGOUS SERIES with the functional group — COOH, which is drawn as ...

$$... -C \begin{matrix} O \\ \\ O-H \end{matrix}$$

The three simplest members of the series are ...

... METHANOIC ACID.

... ETHANOIC ACID.

... PROPANOIC ACID.

Carboxylic acids are found in many substances ...

❶ VINEGAR ...
which contains ETHANOIC ACID.

Ethanoic acid is also used in the manufacture of the fibre, ACETATE RAYON.

❷ ORANGES, LEMONS and MANY SOFT DRINKS ...
... contain CITRIC ACID.

❸ ASPIRIN ...
... is a CARBOXYLIC ACID.

Aspirin is a drug that is used for pain relief and is taken regularly in low dose, by some people to reduce the risk of heart attack.

❹ FRESH FRUIT and VEGETABLES ...
... have ASCORBIC ACID present which is more commonly known as vitamin C.

Reactions Of Carboxylic Acids

Carboxylic acids are weak acids which, like all acids, can be NEUTRALISED by ALKALIS.
They react with CARBONATES and HYDROGENCARBONATES ...
... to produce CARBOXYLIC ACID SALTS, CARBON DIOXIDE and WATER.
For example ...

ETHANOIC ACID + SODIUM CARBONATE ⟶ SODIUM ETHANOATE + CARBON DIOXIDE + WATER

PROPANOIC ACID + POTASSIUM HYDROGENCARBONATE ⟶ POTASSIUM PROPANOATE + CARBON DIOXIDE + WATER

And as we have seen on the previous page, carboxylic acids react with ALCOHOLS to form ESTERS. This reaction is carried out in the presence of CONCENTRATED SULPHURIC ACID which acts as a catalyst.

eg. ETHANOIC ACID + ETHANOL ⟶ ETHYL ETHANOATE + WATER

Most esters are sweet-smelling and for this reason they are often used as FRAGRANCES and FOOD COLOURINGS.

Monomers To Polymers

The majority of POLYMERS (plastics) are made when compounds called MONOMERS which contain the
—C═C— bond join together to form a POLYMER.

When they do so without producing another substance, we call this ADDITION POLYMERISATION
eg. the formation of poly(chloroethene) from chloroethene, CH_2═CHCl, ...

❶ 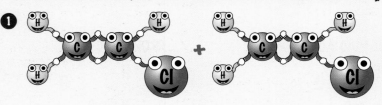   ┼   The small chloroethene molecules
are called MONOMERS.

Their double bonds
are easily broken.

❷    ┼

❸

Therefore large numbers of
molecules can be joined in this way.

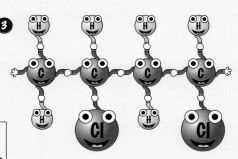

The resulting long chain molecule is a POLYMER - in this case
POLY(CHLOROETHENE) - generally called POLYVINYLCHLORIDE, PVC.

Thermosoftening And Thermosetting Plastics

Polymers (plastics) such as PVC consist of a tangled mass of very long chain molecules where the atoms are
joined by strong covalent bonds. There are two types of plastic.

❶ **THERMOSOFTENING PLASTICS**
In these plastics the chains are held in place by weak
INTERMOLECULAR FORCES. When heated the plastic
softens and the chains can slide over one another
and the plastic can be remoulded over and over again.
When cooled the plastic hardens.
Examples: POLY(ETHENE), POLY(PROPENE) and PVC.

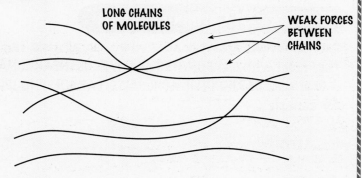

LONG CHAINS
OF MOLECULES

WEAK FORCES
BETWEEN
CHAINS

❷ **THERMOSETTING PLASTICS**

STRONG COVALENT BONDS BETWEEN CHAINS

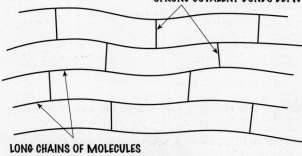

When these plastics are first heated COVALENT BONDS
are formed between adjacent chains. These strong links
mean that thermosetting plastics cannot be softened
on heating and therefore they cannot be re-moulded.
Examples: MELAMINE (used in furniture)
and MANY GLUES.

LONG CHAINS OF MOLECULES

WATER

THE WATER CYCLE

Energy from the SUN causes water in rivers, lakes and oceans to rise via EVAPORATION. As the water vapour rises higher and higher into the atmosphere it cools and condensation occurs forming droplets of water which collect together to form CLOUDS. As the clouds rise further they cool and rain is produced when the droplets are big enough and the whole cycle begins again.

Water is an important raw material and has many uses. These include its use ...

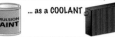 ... as a SOLVENT   ... as a COOLANT   ... in many industrial processes including the manufacture of H_2SO_4.

DRINKING WATER

TWO main steps in producing water which is safe to drink ...

1. The water is passed through a FILTER BED to remove any solid particles.
2. CHLORINE gas is then added to kill any harmful bacteria.

However the use of too much fertiliser results in dissolved NITRATE and AMMONIUM IONS being 'washed out' of the soil into natural waters. This can cause health problems especially for babies.

SOFT AND HARD WATER

Soft water readily forms a lather with soap. Hard water reacts with soap to form SCUM. Therefore more soap is needed to form a lather and deposits called SCALE form in heating systems and kettles. However, hard water is good for your health.

Hard water contains dissolved CALCIUM and MAGNESIUM IONS. These can be removed by ...

1. ... adding SODIUM CARBONATE solution to the hard water.

CALCIUM SULPHATE + SODIUM CARBONATE $\longrightarrow$ SODIUM SULPHATE + CALCIUM CARBONATE

2. ... passing the hard water through an ION-EXCHANGE COLUMN where the calcium and magnesium ions are replaced by hydrogen or sodium ions from the resin in the column.

SOLUBILITY, ACIDIC AND ALKALINE SOLUTIONS

SOLUBILITY OF GASES

Many gases are soluble in water. Their solubility increases as the TEMP. of the water DECREASES and as the PRESSURE on the water INCREASES. Three gases that are soluble are ...

1. CARBON DIOXIDE   2. OXYGEN   3. CHLORINE

SOLUBILITY OF COMPOUNDS

Most IONIC COMPOUNDS are soluble. Most COVALENT COMPOUNDS are insoluble. Solubility is measured in GRAMS OF SOLUTE PER 100grams OF WATER ie. g/100g AT THAT TEMPERATURE.

1. Any point on the curve tells us the maximum amount of copper sulphate that dissolves at a particular water temperature to give us a SATURATED SOLUTION. eg. at 60°C it is 40g/100g of water eg. at 20°C it is 20g/100g of water

2. When a warm saturated solution of copper sulphate cools down some of the copper sulphate will separate from the solution and CRYSTALLISATION occurs eg. if the solution is cooled down from 60°C to 20°C then 40g - 20g = 20g of copper sulphate per 100g of water will crystallise out.

ACIDIC AND ALKALI SOLUTIONS

Some compounds react with water to produce ACIDIC or ALKALINE solutions.

Water must be present for a substance to act as an acid or a base.
- Acids in aqueous sol^n dissociate to produce H^+ ions $HCl_{(aq)} \longrightarrow H^+_{(aq)} + Cl^-_{(aq)}$
- Alkalis in aqueous sol^n dissociate to produce OH^- ions $NaOH_{(aq)} \longrightarrow Na^+_{(aq)} + OH^-_{(aq)}$
- Arrhenius proposed that aqueous solutions of acids contain $H^+_{(aq)}$ ions.
- Brönsted suggested that an ACID is a proton donor and a BASE is a proton acceptor.

STRENGTH OF ACIDS AND ALKALIS

A STRONG ACID or ALKALI is one that is 100% ionised in water. WEAK ACIDS or ALKALIS are only partially ionised.
- Different acids of the same concentration can have different pH values. It depends on the extent of their ionisation. Consequently strong acids have a low pH.
- The strength of acids can also be distinguished by their rate of reaction with METALS.

PRODUCING SALTS

Here are five typical ways of producing them ...

1. REACTING A METAL WITH AN ACID.
eg. MAGNESIUM + SULPHURIC ACID $\longrightarrow$ MAGNESIUM SULPHATE + HYDROGEN
$Mg_{(s)}$ + $H_2SO_{4(aq)}$ $\longrightarrow$ $MgSO_{4(aq)}$ + $H_{2(g)}$

2. REACTING AN INSOLUBLE BASE WITH AN ACID
eg. COPPER OXIDE + SULPHURIC ACID $\longrightarrow$ COPPER SULPHATE + WATER
$CuO_{(s)}$ + $H_2SO_{4(aq)}$ $\longrightarrow$ $CuSO_{4(aq)}$ + $H_2O_{(l)}$

3. REACTING A SOLUBLE BASE WITH AN ACID
eg. HYDROCHLORIC ACID + SODIUM HYDROXIDE $\longrightarrow$ SODIUM CHLORIDE + WATER
$HCl_{(aq)}$ + $NaOH_{(aq)}$ $\longrightarrow$ $NaCl_{(aq)}$ + $H_2O_{(l)}$

4. MIXING TWO SOLUTIONS TO FORM AN INSOLUBLE SALT (PRECIPITATION)
eg. BARIUM CHLORIDE + SODIUM SULPHATE $\longrightarrow$ BARIUM SULPHATE + SODIUM CHLORIDE
$BaCl_{2(aq)}$ + $Na_2SO_{4(aq)}$ $\longrightarrow$ $BaSO_{4(s)}$ + $NaCl_{(aq)}$

5. DIRECT COMBINATION OF THE ELEMENTS TO FORM ANHYDROUS SALTS
eg. IRON + CHLORINE $\longrightarrow$ IRON (III) CHLORIDE
$2Fe_{(s)}$ + $3Cl_{2(g)}$ $\longrightarrow$ $2FeCl_{3(s)}$

NB You need to be familiar with the practical details of all of the above ways of producing salts.

TITRATION

This is an accurate technique to find out how much of an acid is needed to neutralise an alkali.

- A PIPETTE is used to measure out a known and accurate volume of the alkali. A suitable indicator is added to it.
- A BURETTE is used to carefully add acid to the alkali until the indicator changes colour to show neutrality. The volume of acid added can be measured from the burette readings.

CLAMP
BURETTE
ACID
ALKALI + INDICATOR

THE MOLE, CONC^N OF SOLUTIONS AND TITRATION CALCULATIONS

THE MOLE

- A MOLE (mol) is a measure of the number of 'particles' contained in a substance. One mole of any substance contains the same number of particles.
- The MASS of ONE MOLE of a substance called the MOLAR MASS (g/mol) is always equal to the RELATIVE ATOMIC MASS, Ar, or RELATIVE FORMULA MASS, Mr, of that substance (element or compound) in grams.

eg. aluminium 27g/mol 1m   sulphur 32g/mol 1m   sodium hydroxide 40g/mol 1m

$$\text{NUMBER OF MOLES OF SUBSTANCE (mol)} = \frac{\text{MASS OF SUBSTANCE (g)}}{\text{MASS OF ONE MOLE (g/mol)}}$$

CONCENTRATION OF SOLUTIONS

The CONCENTRATION of an aqueous solution is usually expressed by stating how many MOLES of a particular solute are present in each CUBIC DECIMETRE of solution. Concentration is measured in moles per cubic decimetre (mol dm^{-3} or M). One cubic decimetre is the same as 1000cm^3 or 1 litre. If we take a solution that has a concentration of ...

... 1mol dm^{-3} ... then 1mol of solute is present in every 1dm^3 of solution

... 0.5mol dm^{-3} ... then 0.5mol of solute is present in every 1dm^3 of solution

... 2mol dm^{-3} ... then 2mol of solute is present in every 1dm^3 of solution

$$\text{CONCENTRATION OF SOLUTION (mol dm}^{-3}\text{ or M)} = \frac{\text{NUMBER OF MOLES OF SOLUTE (mol)}}{\text{VOLUME OF SOLUTION (dm}^3\text{)}}$$

TITRATION CALCULATIONS

TITRATION can be used to find the CONC^N of an ACID or ALKALI providing we know the relative volumes of acid and alkali used and the CONC^N of either the acid or the alkali.

STAGE 1 – From the given balanced equation you will be able to determine the ratio of number of moles of acid to alkali for the reaction taking place.

STAGE 2 – Calculate the number of moles in the solution of known volume and concentration. You will now know the number of moles in the other solution from stage 1.

STAGE 3 – Calculate the concentration of the other solution.

ORGANIC COMPOUNDS, HOMOLOGOUS SERIES AND ISOMERISM

BURNING ORGANIC COMPOUNDS

AN ORGANIC COMPOUND is simply a substance that contains CARBON. With COMPLETE COMBUSTION the products are CARBON DIOXIDE and WATER.
eg. METHANE + OXYGEN $\longrightarrow$ CARBON DIOXIDE + WATER

With INCOMPLETE COMBUSTION the products are CARBON MONOXIDE/CARBON and WATER.
eg. METHANE + OXYGEN $\longrightarrow$ CARBON MONOXIDE + WATER
eg. METHANE + OXYGEN $\longrightarrow$ CARBON + WATER

Different fossil fuels produce different amounts of energy when burnt.

BURNING PLASTICS AND OTHER ORGANIC COMPOUNDS

- HYDROGEN CHLORIDE is produced if the compound contains CHLORINE; HYDROGEN CYANIDE is produced if the compound contains NITROGEN.

HOMOLOGOUS SERIES

A HOMOLOGOUS SERIES is a family of compounds which have a GENERAL FORMULA and have SIMILAR CHEMICAL PROPERTIES.
- The ALKANES have a general formula C_nH_{2n+2} where n = 1, 2, 3, 4 and so on.
- The ALKENES have a general formula C_nH_{2n} where n = 2, 3, 4, 5 and so on.

ADDITION REACTIONS OF ALKENES
Alkenes are more reactive than alkanes.

1. ETHENE + HYDROGEN $\longrightarrow$ ETHANE
2. ETHENE + BROMINE $\longrightarrow$ COLOURLESS PRODUCT

ISOMERS

Isomerism occurs when two or more compounds have the same chemical formula but different structures. The physical properties of an isomer depend on the intermolecular forces of attraction between neighbouring isomers. Long chain isomers have HIGHER BOILING POINTS than isomers where the chain is branched.

ALCOHOLS, CARBOXYLIC ACIDS AND POLYMERS

ETHANOL

ETHANOL can be used as a SOLVENT, FUEL, or component in ALCOHOLIC DRINKS. It can be produced by ...

... the FERMENTATION OF SUGARS

... reacting STEAM with ETHENE at a moderately high temp. and pressure in the presence of the catalyst, phosphoric acid.   ETHENE + STEAM $\xrightarrow{\text{phosphoric acid}}$ ETHANOL

REACTIONS OF ALCOHOLS

Alcohols form a HOMOLOGOUS SERIES with the functional group $-OH$.
- They react reversibly with CARBOXYLIC ACIDS to form ESTERS and WATER.
- They react with SODIUM to form HYDROGEN.
Cholesterol, a steroid, contains the alcohol group $-OH$.

CARBOXYLIC ACIDS

These form a HOMOLOGOUS SERIES with the functional group $-COOH$. They are found in VINEGAR, ORANGES, LEMONS, SOFT DRINKS, ASPIRIN and FRESH FRUIT and VEGETABLES.

REACTIONS OF CARBOXYLIC ACIDS

- They are NEUTRALISED by ALKALIS.
- They react with CARBONATES and HYDROGENCARBONATES to produce CARBOXYLIC ACID SALTS, CARBON DIOXIDE AND WATER.
eg. ETHANOIC ACID + SODIUM CARBONATE $\longrightarrow$ SODIUM ETHANOATE + CARBON DIOXIDE + WATER

POLYMERS

POLYMERS are made when MONOMERS which contain the $-C = C-$ bond join together. It is called ADDITION POLYMERISATION when they do so without producing another substance.

- THERMOSOFTENING PLASTICS can be re-moulded again and again as the chains in these plastics are held in place by weak intermolecular forces.
- THERMOSETTING PLASTICS cannot be re-moulded as strong covalent bonds are formed between adjacent chains.

1. Choose words from the list for each of the spaces 1–4 to complete the sentences below.
   A. NITROGEN.
   B. HAEMOGLOBIN.
   C. NITRATE.
   D. FERTILISERS.

   Artificial __1__ can be used to replace the __2__ in the soil used up by previous crops. However, too much fertiliser results in dissolved __3__ ions being washed out of the soil into rivers and lakes. These ions can reduce the ability of __4__ to carry oxygen.

2. The table below is about hard and soft water. Match words from the list with each of the numbers 1–4 in the table.
   A. HARD WATER.
   B. SCALE.
   C. SOFT WATER.
   D. ION-EXCHANGE COLUMN.

1	A deposit formed in heating systems and kettles caused by hard water.
2	A device for making hard water soft.
3	Water which contains low levels of dissolved calcium and magnesium compounds.
4	Water which contains high levels of dissolved calcium or magnesium compounds.

3. This question concerns solubility of gases. Which TWO of the following statements are true? Solubility of gases in water ...
   A ... increases as temperature decreases and pressure increases.
   B ... decreases as temperature decreases and pressure increases.
   C ... decreases as temperature increases and pressure decreases.
   D ... increases as temperature and pressure decrease.
   E ... decreases as temperature and pressure increase.

4. Some compounds react with water to produce acidic or alkaline solutions.

   4.1 All acids in aqueous solution
   A. Produce various ions.
   B. Produce hydroxide ions.
   C. Produce hydrogen ions.
   D. Produce hydrogen atoms.

   4.2 All alkalis in aqueous solution
   A. Produce various ions.
   B. Produce hydroxide ions.
   C. Produce hydrogen ions.
   D. Produce hydrogen atoms.

   4.3 The Danish chemist Brönsted defined acids as
   A. PROTON ACCEPTORS.
   B. HYDROGEN ION ACCEPTORS.
   C. PROTON DONORS.
   D. HYDROGEN DONORS.

   4.4 Brönsted also defined alkalis as
   A. PROTON ACCEPTORS.
   B. HYDROGEN ACCEPTORS.
   C. PROTON DONORS.
   D. HYDROGEN ION DONORS.

5. This question involves various calculations for which a calculator is necessary.

   5.1 How many moles of sulphur are in 640 grams of the element if its molar mass is 32g?
   A. 0.05
   B. 200
   C. 20
   D. 608

   5.2 What is the concentration of an aqueous solution if 7 mol of solute is present in 0.25 dm³ of solution?
   A. 7.25mol dm^{-3}
   B. 1.75mol dm^{-3}
   C. 0.035mol dm^{-3}
   D. 28mol dm^{-3}

   5.3 What is the concentration of an aqueous solution of 192g of sodium hydroxide in 3000cm³ of water. (Rel. formula mass of NaOH is 40)?
   A. 1.6mol dm^{-3}
   B. 0.0016mol dm^{-3}
   C. 0.064mol dm^{-3}
   D. 64mol dm^{-3}

   5.4 What is the concentration of 0.06dm³ of hydrochloric acid which exactly neutralises 0.18dm³ of sodium hydroxide of concentration 0.5mol dm^{-3}?
   A. 1.49mol dm^{-3}
   B. 0.166mol dm^{-3}
   C. 1.5mol dm^{-3}
   D. 15mol dm^{-3}

6. Hydrocarbons are compounds formed from carbon and hydrogen atoms.

   6.1 Which substances are formed during the complete combustion of methane?
   A. CARBON AND WATER.
   B. CARBON DIOXIDE AND WATER.
   C. CARBON MONOXIDE AND WATER.
   D. CARBON MONOXIDE AND CARBON DIOXIDE.

   6.2 Which of the following substances is an alkene?
   A. C_2H_6
   B. C_3H_8
   C. C_4H_{10}
   D. C_5H_{10}

   6.3 Which of the following hydrocarbons would both decolourise bromine water.
   A. METHANE AND ETHENE.
   B. ETHANE AND BUTANE.
   C. PROPENE AND BUTENE.
   D. PENTENE AND PROPANE.

   6.4 Which of the following statements is true of the intermolecular forces between isomers?
   A. They increase as the chain length increases resulting in higher boiling points.
   B. They decrease as the chain length increases resulting in lower boiling points.
   C. They increase as the chain length increases resulting in lower boiling points.
   D. They decrease as the chain length decreases resulting in higher boiling points.

7. This question is about alcohols and carboxylic acids.

   7.1 When yeast ferments sugar solution (anaerobically) the products formed are ...
   A. CARBON DIOXIDE AND WATER.
   B. ETHANOL AND WATER.
   C. ETHANOL AND CARBON DIOXIDE.
   D. ETHANOL AND OXYGEN.

   7.2 Ethanol can be produced industrially by reacting which of the following substances?
   A. SUGAR AND STEAM.
   B. SUGAR AND CARBON DIOXIDE.
   C. CARBON DIOXIDE AND STEAM.
   D. ETHENE AND STEAM.

   7.3 Which one of the following substances is not a carboxylic acid?

   A. [structure: H–C(=O)–O–H]
   B. [structure: H–C–C–C–C(=O)–O–H, with H atoms]
   C. [structure: H–C(=O)–O–H]
   D. [structure: H₂C=CH–O–H]

   7.4 Which one of the following substances is a carboxylic acid?
   A. NITRIC ACID.
   B. HYDROCHLORIC ACID.
   C. CITRIC ACID.
   D. SULPHURIC ACID.

A switch is a device that controls the flow of current in an electric circuit.

If we have a circuit containing a cell, a switch and a lamp ...

When the switch is CLOSED (ON) ...

When the switch is OPEN (OFF) ...

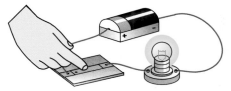

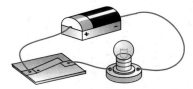

... a current will flow through the lamp.

... a current doesn't flow through the lamp.

In other words for the lamp to be 'ON' it must be part of a complete circuit ...

... otherwise it is 'OFF'.

How Switches Control Devices In Simple Circuits

The following FOUR SERIES CIRCUITS each contain a cell, two lamps (A and B) and three switches ...

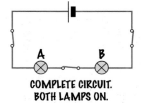

COMPLETE CIRCUIT.
BOTH LAMPS ON.

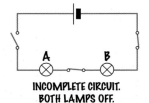

INCOMPLETE CIRCUIT.
BOTH LAMPS OFF.

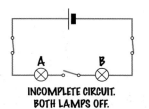

INCOMPLETE CIRCUIT.
BOTH LAMPS OFF.

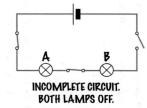

INCOMPLETE CIRCUIT.
BOTH LAMPS OFF.

You will notice that in a series circuit the two lamps are either both ON or both OFF, ...

... it is not possible to have one lamp on and the other off.

The following FOUR PARALLEL CIRCUITS each contain a cell, two lamps (A and B) and three switches ...

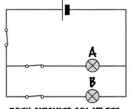

BOTH CIRCUITS COMPLETE.
BOTH LAMPS ON.

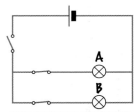

BOTH CIRCUITS INCOMPLETE.
BOTH LAMPS OFF.

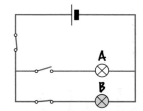

CIRCUIT 'A' INCOMPLETE, LAMP 'A' OFF.
CIRCUIT 'B' COMPLETE, LAMP 'B' ON.

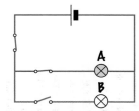

CIRCUIT 'A' COMPLETE, LAMP 'A' ON.
CIRCUIT 'B' INCOMPLETE, LAMP 'B' OFF.

This time you will notice that the lamps can be either both ON or both OFF ...

... or they can be INDIVIDUALLY SWITCHED ON or OFF if they are in their own loop.

The Relay

A relay is a switch which allows a SMALLER CURRENT ...

... to switch on a LARGER CURRENT for safety.

The symbol for a relay (normally open) is shown opposite.

Below is a very simple diagram of how a relay works ...

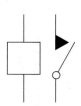

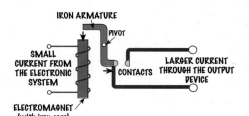

- A small current from the electronic system ...
    ... flows through the coil of the relay ...
    ... and the electromagnet is switched ON.
- The pivoted iron armature is pulled towards ...
    ... the electromagnet causing the contacts to close ...
    ... which switches on a larger current through the output device.

Fixed And Variable Resistors

The flow of current through a circuit can be controlled by using ...

❶ ... a FIXED RESISTOR

A fixed resistor is a component whose resistance is constant. The bigger its resistance the smaller the current that flows for a particular voltage. Resistance is measured in ohms (Ω).

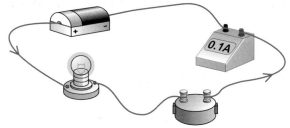

FIXED RESISTOR with a high resistance

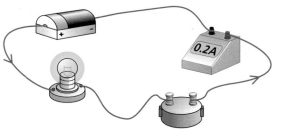

FIXED RESISTOR with a low resistance

❷ ... a VARIABLE RESISTOR

A variable resistor is a component whose resistance can be altered. The current that flows can be changed by simply moving the sliding contact of the variable resistor from one end to the other as shown below.

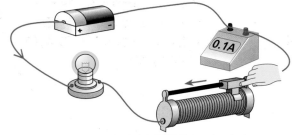

VARIABLE RESISTOR with a high resistance.

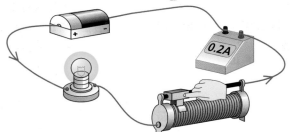

VARIABLE RESISTOR with a low resistance.

Resistor Colour Code

Resistors that are commonly used in electronic equipment are often colour coded with four bands (though some may only have three). These bands tell us the value of the RESISTANCE and TOLERANCE (an allowable variation in the value of the resistance).

The FIRST TWO BANDS represent the FIRST TWO DIGITS of the resistance.

THE THIRD BAND represents the number of ZEROS there are after the first two digits....

... and the FOURTH BAND represents the tolerance as a percentage.

	BANDS 1, 2, AND 3										BAND 4		
COLOUR	BLACK	BROWN	RED	ORANGE	YELLOW	GREEN	BLUE	VIOLET	GREY	WHITE	COLOUR	GOLD	SILVER	NO BAND
NUMBER	0	1	2	3	4	5	6	7	8	9	TOLERANCE	5%	10%	20%

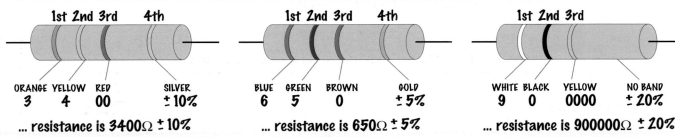

1st 2nd 3rd	4th
ORANGE YELLOW RED	SILVER
3 4 00	± 10%

... resistance is 3400Ω ± 10%

1st 2nd 3rd	4th
BLUE GREEN BROWN	GOLD
6 5 0	± 5%

... resistance is 650Ω ± 5%

1st 2nd 3rd	
WHITE BLACK YELLOW	NO BAND
9 0 0000	± 20%

... resistance is 900000Ω ± 20%

A very simple electronic system consists of three stages ...

ONE OR MORE INPUT SENSORS	→	A PROCESSOR	→	AN OUTPUT DEVICE

... which detect if there is a change in the environment.

... which acts as a decision maker and decides what action is needed.

... which is controlled by the output from the processor.

Input Sensors

These are energy changers where a NON-ELECTRICAL INPUT causes an ELECTRICAL OUTPUT. Input sensors include ...

... THERMISTORS which detect any change in temperature. As the temperature rises the resistance decreases which allows a flow of electric current.

... LIGHT DEPENDENT RESISTORS (LDR) which detect any change in light intensity. As the light intensity rises its resistance decreases which allows a flow of electric current.

... SWITCHES which usually complete a circuit. Mechanical energy enables an electric current to flow in a circuit. Can be used to respond to • PRESSURE • TILTING • MAGNETIC FIELD • MOISTURE

Output Devices

These are also energy changers where an ELECTRICAL INPUT causes a NON-ELECTRICAL OUTPUT. All the following output devices convert ELECTRICAL ENERGY into various other forms of energy.

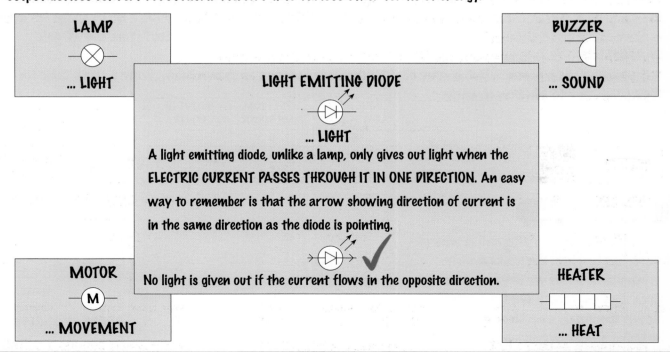

LAMP
... LIGHT

BUZZER
... SOUND

LIGHT EMITTING DIODE
... LIGHT
A light emitting diode, unlike a lamp, only gives out light when the ELECTRIC CURRENT PASSES THROUGH IT IN ONE DIRECTION. An easy way to remember is that the arrow showing direction of current is in the same direction as the diode is pointing.

No light is given out if the current flows in the opposite direction.

MOTOR
... MOVEMENT

HEATER
... HEAT

Processors

A processor is a decision maker. LOGIC GATES and TRANSISTORS (see p40) are processors. They work using digital information where the input(s) into and output from are one of two states: ON (or 1 or HIGH) or OFF (or 0 or LOW). An ON (or 1 or HIGH) state is a voltage close to the supply voltage while an OFF (or 0 or LOW) is a voltage close to zero. With digital information there are no 'in between' values, only two states exist. The three logic gates you need to know are called AND, OR and NOT. How they behave can be shown in a TRUTH TABLE.

LOGIC GATE	SYMBOL	WHAT HAPPENS	TRUTH TABLE		
AND	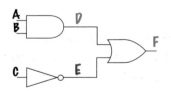	The output is ON or 1 if the first input AND the second input are both ON or 1. Otherwise the output is OFF or 0.	First input	Second input	Output
			0	0	0
			1	0	0
			0	1	0
			1	1	1
OR		The output is ON or 1 if the first input OR the second input OR both inputs are ON or 1. Otherwise the output is OFF or 0.	First input	Second input	Output
			0	0	0
			1	0	1
			0	1	1
			1	1	1
NOT		The output is ON or 1 if the input is NOT ON or 1 and vice versa.	Input	Output	
			0	1	
			1	0	

You will be expected to be able to use truth tables to determine the output of a combination of not more than 3 gates and also use them to represent appropriate problems stated in words (maximum 3 inputs).

EXAMPLE 1

Draw a truth table for the following logic circuit

A	B	C	D	E	F
0	0	0	0	1	1
1	0	1	0	0	0
0	1	0	0	1	1
1	1	1	1	0	1

NB

'D' is the output from the AND gate ...
... and the FIRST INPUT to the OR gate.
'E' is the output from the NOT gate ...
... and the SECOND INPUT to the OR gate.
'F' is the output from the OR gate.

EXAMPLE 2

A greenhouse has a heater which is controlled by two input sensors as shown below. Draw a truth table for the system and explain how it works.

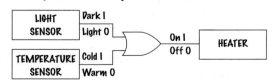

INPUT FROM LIGHT SENSOR	INPUT FROM TEMP. SENSOR	OUTPUT TO HEATER
0	0	0
1	0	1
0	1	1
1	1	1

From the truth table the heater is switched on when it becomes dark or it becomes cold. A useful system in winter?

Block Diagrams

A block diagram is an alternative way of describing a simple electronic system. In example 2 above we have a mixture of block diagrams and a symbol. Example 2, drawn completely as a block diagram, including a relay, would look like this ...

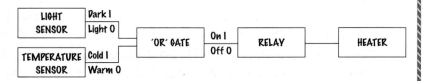

THE POTENTIAL DIVIDER

How A Potential Divider Works

A very simple POTENTIAL DIVIDER (ie. a voltage divider) consists of an INPUT VOLTAGE, V_{in}, which is applied ACROSS TWO RESISTORS, R_1 and R_2, arranged in series. The input voltage, V_{in}, is shared across the two resistors with the voltage across the lower resistor, V_{out}, being 'tapped off' to become the INPUT VOLTAGE across a PROCESSOR.

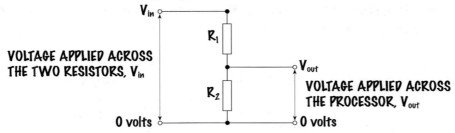

Providing we know the value of V_{in}, R_1 and R_2 then V_{out} can be calculated using the following equation ...

$$V_{out} = V_{in} \times \frac{(R_2)}{(R_1 + R_2)}$$

If the resistance of either resistor is increased (or decreased) then the voltage across that resistor also increases (or decreases). This will alter the value of V_{out}, for example ...

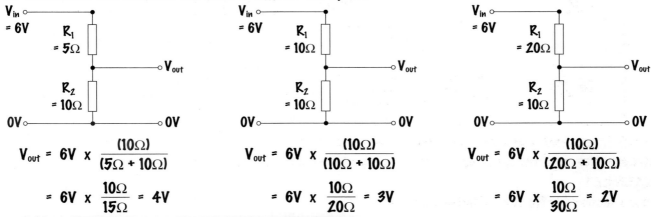

$$V_{out} = 6V \times \frac{(10\Omega)}{(5\Omega + 10\Omega)} = 6V \times \frac{10\Omega}{15\Omega} = 4V$$

$$V_{out} = 6V \times \frac{(10\Omega)}{(10\Omega + 10\Omega)} = 6V \times \frac{10\Omega}{20\Omega} = 3V$$

$$V_{out} = 6V \times \frac{(10\Omega)}{(20\Omega + 10\Omega)} = 6V \times \frac{10\Omega}{30\Omega} = 2V$$

Practical Application Of A Potential Divider

In practice the two resistors, R_1 and R_2, are an INPUT SENSOR (eg. an LDR, thermistor) and a VARIABLE RESISTOR. The resistance of the input sensor changes as its surroundings change which results in V_{out} changing. If V_{out} changes enough then the input to the processor will also change from HIGH to LOW (or vice versa). If we take our input sensor to be an LDR ...

If the light intensity DECREASES ...
... then the resistance of the LDR INCREASES ...
... in comparison to the resistance of the variable resistor.
This causes V_{out} to DECREASE ...
... and the INPUT to the processor ...
... will change from HIGH to LOW.

If the light intensity INCREASES ...
... then the resistance of the LDR DECREASES ...
... in comparison to the resistance of the variable resistor.
This causes V_{out} to INCREASE ...
... and the INPUT to the processor ...
... will change from LOW to HIGH.

NB The resistance of the VARIABLE RESISTOR can be adjusted so that V_{out} changes from HIGH to LOW (and vice versa) when the surroundings that the input sensor detects are at a particular level. This allows the user to determine the conditions which will switch on the output device.

Below is a symbol circuit diagram for an electronic system that can be used as a **LIGHT DEPENDENT SWITCH**. The output device is switched on when the light intensity **DECREASES** to a certain level....

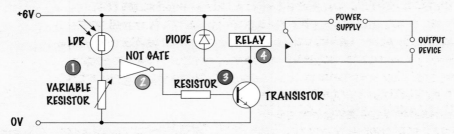

How the circuit works can be split into four stages ...

① As the **LIGHT INTENSITY DECREASES** the resistance of the LDR increases in comparison to the resistance of the variable resistor. This causes the **VOLTAGE** across the **VARIABLE RESISTOR** to **DECREASE** ...

② ... until the **NOT GATE** recognises this input to be **LOW** (or OFF) in which case the gate inverts it to a **HIGH** (or ON) which causes a current to flow ...

③ ... into the **TRANSISTOR** via a **RESISTOR** which reduces the amount of current flowing (in order to prevent damage to the transistor). The transistor simply acts as a **SWITCH** ...

④ ... allowing a small current to flow into the **RELAY** which switches on the larger current needed for the **OUTPUT DEVICE** eg. a lamp. Across the relay is a reverse biased **DIODE** which protects the transistor by acting as a buffer when the relay is switched off.

Modifying The Above Circuit

The above circuit can be modified so that the **OUTPUT DEVICE** is switched on at a **DIFFERENT LIGHT INTENSITY**. This can be done by simply adjusting the resistance of the variable resistor. If we decrease its resistance then the light intensity need not fall to a level as low as above before the voltage across the variable resistor decreases sufficiently to be a **LOW** input for the NOT gate and vice versa.

Also, by simply swapping the positions of the LDR and variable resistor it becomes an electronic system which does the opposite of above ie. the output device is switched on when the **LIGHT INTENSITY INCREASES** to a certain level.

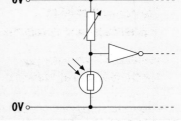

Capacitors

A CAPACITOR is a CHARGE STORER; just like a battery, only in most cases it's temporary. If a current 'flows into' an uncharged capacitor, charge is stored on the capacitor and the voltage or potential difference (p.d.) across the capacitor increases. However the maximum p.d. across the capacitor cannot be greater than the supply voltage which means that there is a limit to the amount of charge that can be stored.

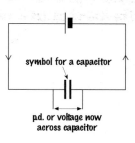

symbol for a capacitor

p.d. or voltage now across capacitor

Charging And Discharging Capacitors

Any circuit which has a capacitor in it will also have RESISTANCE (other components, wires etc.) where ...
... the GREATER the RESISTANCE of the charging or discharging circuit ...
... and the GREATER the value of the CAPACITOR ...
... the LONGER it takes for the CAPACITOR to CHARGE or DISCHARGE.

If we CHARGE a capacitor ...   If we DISCHARGE a capacitor ...

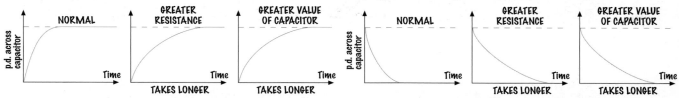

A capacitor can be used as a TIMER in an electronic system that needs to be activated for a set period of time.

Capacitor As A Time Delay Switch

A capacitor can be used as the 'INPUT SENSOR' for a TIME DELAY SWITCH. If we take the following circuit which is slightly modified from the circuit on page 40, ...

IF SWITCH S IS CLOSED ...

The CAPACITOR has no p.d. across it since it is being short-circuited by the CLOSED SWITCH, S. The input to the NOT GATE is LOW (or 0) resulting in its output being HIGH (or 1). The TRANSISTOR is switched 'on' which causes the RELAY contacts to close and the OUTPUT DEVICE IS SWITCHED ON.

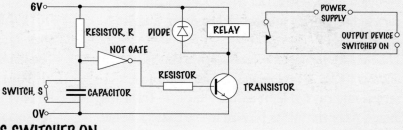

IF SWITCH S IS OPENED ...

The CAPACITOR will start to CHARGE UP (as it is no longer being short-circuited). However a TIME DELAY occurs before the p.d. across the capacitor increases sufficiently for the NOT GATE to recognise this input as HIGH (or 1) to give an output of LOW (or 0.) The TRANSISTOR is now switched 'off' which causes the RELAY contacts to open and the OUTPUT DEVICE IS SWITCHED OFF.

NB The TIME DELAY can be increased by increasing the resistance of resistor, R, or by increasing the value of the capacitor.

Advantages And Disadvantages Of Using Electronic Systems

As with any other technology, using electronic systems has its advantages and its disadvantages, for example ...

CCTV ...	MOBILE PHONES ...	INTERNET ...
👍 Benefits of SECURITY against theft and vandalism.	👍 Benefits for WORKING PRACTICES.	👍 Benefits of its EDUCATIONAL VALUE.
👎 Drawback in its potential for the invasion of PRIVACY.	👎 Drawback in their potential for INTRUSION and HEALTH HAZARDS.	👎 Drawback of allowing UNSUITABLE MATERIAL to be transmitted to children.

Converging And Diverging Lenses

There are TWO types of lens:

1 CONVERGING (or convex)
A converging lens is thickest at its centre.
eg.

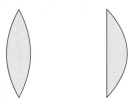

2 DIVERGING (or concave)
A diverging lens is thinnest at its centre.
eg.

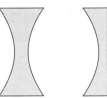

Due to this difference in curvature, PARALLEL RAYS of light pass differently through them.

With a CONVERGING LENS ...

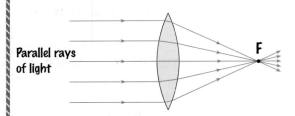

Parallel rays of light

... the rays of light (with the exception of the middle one which meets the lens at 90° and passes straight through) are REFRACTED INWARDS at the two curved boundaries to meet at one point, F, called the FOCUS.
The IMAGE formed by a converging lens is nearly always REAL. A real image can be formed on a screen and rays of light actually meet to form the image, as in the image formed in the camera below.

With a DIVERGING LENS ...

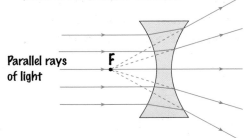

Parallel rays of light

... the rays of light (again, with the exception of the middle one which meets the lens at 90° and passes straight through) are REFRACTED OUTWARDS at the two curved boundaries so that they appear to come from one point, F, the FOCUS.
The IMAGE formed by a diverging lens is always VIRTUAL. A virtual image cannot be formed on a screen and rays of light only appear to come from the image.

The Camera

The diagram below shows a converging lens in a camera being used to produce an image of an object on photographic film.

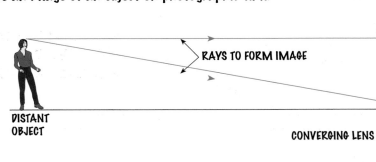

RAYS TO FORM IMAGE

DISTANT OBJECT

CONVERGING LENS

PHOTOGRAPHIC FILM

IMAGE

The image formed ...
• ... is SMALLER than the object, and ...
• ... is NEARER to the LENS, compared to the object.

Construction Of Ray Diagrams

Ray diagrams can be used to show the formation of the image by a converging lens. If they are drawn accurately then information about the position, nature and size of the image, as compared to the object, can be determined. To construct a ray diagram TWO rays of light need to be drawn from the top of the object ...

- The FIRST RAY goes parallel to the axis and is then refracted through the FOCUS, F.

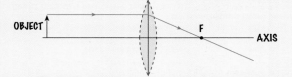

- The SECOND RAY goes straight through the centre of the lens and is UNDEVIATED.

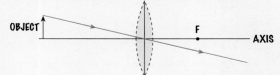

Ray Diagrams For Converging Lenses

For a converging lens the image formed depends on the position of the object. Two important positions on the axis, on both sides of the lens, are F and 2F. (2F is a position that is twice as far away from the centre of the lens as F is.) There are FIVE possible ray diagrams ...

POSITION OF OBJECT	RAY DIAGRAM	PROPERTIES OF IMAGE
BEYOND 2F		• REAL • UPSIDE DOWN • SMALLER THAN OBJECT
AT 2F		• REAL • UPSIDE DOWN • SAME SIZE AS OBJECT
BETWEEN 2F AND F		• REAL • UPSIDE DOWN • LARGER THAN OBJECT
AT F		• Since the two rays are parallel and will never meet we say that the image is formed at INFINITY.
BETWEEN F AND THE LENS		• VIRTUAL (the odd one out) • RIGHT WAY UP • LARGER THAN OBJECT

Two important points:

1 The position of the object as shown in the top diagram ie. BEYOND 2F is the arrangement used in cameras.

2 The position of the object as shown in the bottom diagram ie. BETWEEN F AND THE LENS is the arrangement used in magnifying glasses.

SWITCHES AND RESISTORS

SWITCHES
A switch is a device that controls the flow of current in an electrical circuit.
Switches can be used to control devices in simple circuits.
In a SERIES circuit ...

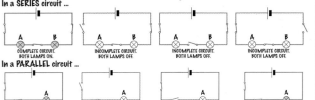

COMPLETE CIRCUIT. BOTH LAMPS ON. | INCOMPLETE CIRCUIT. BOTH LAMPS OFF. | INCOMPLETE CIRCUIT. BOTH LAMPS OFF. | INCOMPLETE CIRCUIT. BOTH LAMPS OFF.

In a PARALLEL circuit ...

BOTH CIRCUITS COMPLETE. BOTH LAMPS ON. | BOTH CIRCUITS INCOMPLETE. BOTH LAMPS OFF. | CIRCUIT 'A' INCOMPLETE, LAMP 'A' OFF. CIRCUIT 'B' COMPLETE, LAMP 'B' ON. | CIRCUIT 'A' COMPLETE, LAMP 'A' ON. CIRCUIT 'B' INCOMPLETE, LAMP 'B' OFF.

THE RELAY
A RELAY is a switch which allows a SMALLER current to switch on a larger current for safety.

FIXED AND VARIABLE RESISTORS
A fixed resistor is a component whose resistance is constant.
The bigger its resistance the smaller the current that flows for
a particular voltage. Resistance is measured in ohms (Ω).
• A variable resistor is a component ...
... whose resistance can be altered.

VARIABLE RESISTOR ...
... with a high resistance.

RESISTOR COLOUR CODE
Resistors are often colour coded with four bands (some may have only three). These bands tell us the value
of its RESISTANCE and TOLERANCE. The FIRST TWO BANDS represent the first TWO DIGITS of the
resistance. The THIRD BAND represents the number of ZEROS there are after the first two digits.
The FOURTH BAND represents the TOLERANCE.

ELECTRONIC SYSTEMS

INPUT SENSORS
These are energy changers where a NON-ELECTRICAL INPUT causes an ELECTRICAL OUTPUT.

THERMISTORS detect any change in temperature. As the temperature rises the resistance decreases which allows a flow of electric current.

LIGHT DEPENDENT RESISTORS (LDR) detect any change in light intensity. As the light intensity rises its resistance decreases which allows a flow of electric current.

SWITCHES usually complete a circuit. Mechanical energy enables an electric current to flow in a circuit. Can be used to respond to • PRESSURE • TILTING • MAGNETIC FIELD • MOISTURE

OUTPUT DEVICES
These are energy changers where an ELECTRICAL INPUT causes a NON-ELECTRICAL OUTPUT.
The following convert electrical energy into ...

LAMP ... LIGHT | BUZZER ... SOUND | LIGHT EMITTING DIODE ... LIGHT | MOTOR ... MOVEMENT | HEATER ... HEAT

PROCESSORS
A PROCESSOR is a decision
maker. LOGIC GATES are
processors and how they behave
can be shown in a TRUTH TABLE.

BLOCK DIAGRAMS
A block diagram describes a
simple electronic system.

LOGIC GATE	SYMBOL	TRUTH TABLE		
AND		First input	Second input	Output
		0	0	0
		1	0	0
		0	1	0
		1	1	1
OR		First input	Second input	Output
		0	0	0
		1	0	1
		0	1	1
		1	1	1
NOT		Input	Output	
		0	1	
		1	0	

THE POTENTIAL DIVIDER

THE POTENTIAL DIVIDER
A POTENTIAL DIVIDER consists of an INPUT VOLTAGE, V_{in}, which is applied across two resistors, R_1 and
R_2, arranged in series. V_{in} is shared across the two resistors where the voltage across the lower resistor,
V_{out} becomes the INPUT VOLTAGE across a PROCESSOR.

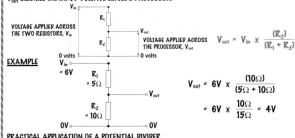

VOLTAGE APPLIED ACROSS
THE TWO RESISTORS, V_{in}

VOLTAGE APPLIED ACROSS
THE PROCESSOR V_{out}

$$V_{out} = V_{in} \times \frac{(R_2)}{(R_1 + R_2)}$$

EXAMPLE
$V_{in} = 6V$
$R_1 = 5\Omega$
$R_2 = 10\Omega$

$$V_{out} = 6V \times \frac{(10\Omega)}{(5\Omega + 10\Omega)}$$

$$= 6V \times \frac{10\Omega}{15\Omega} = 4V$$

PRACTICAL APPLICATION OF A POTENTIAL DIVIDER
Input to processor is HIGH ...

... changes from
HIGH to LOW.

If the light intensity DECREASES ...
... then the resistance of the LDR INCREASES ...
... in comparison to the resistance of the variable resistor.
This causes V_{out} to DECREASE ...
... and the INPUT to the processor ...
... will change from HIGH to LOW.

The resistance of the variable resistor can be adjusted so that V_{out} changes from HIGH to LOW (or vice
versa) when the surroundings that the input sensor detects are at a particular level.

ELECTRONIC SYSTEMS IN ACTION

EXAMPLE

+6V | LDR | NOT GATE | DIODE | RELAY | POWER SUPPLY | OUTPUT DEVICE
VARIABLE RESISTOR | RESISTOR | TRANSISTOR
0V

MODIFYING THE ABOVE CIRCUIT
• Altering the resistance of the
variable resistor causes the
output device to be switched on at
a different light intensity.
• Swapping the positions of the LDR
and variable resistor causes it to
become an electronic system which
does the opposite of above.

① As the LIGHT INTENSITY DECREASES the resistance of the LDR
increases in comparison to the resistance of the variable resistor.
This causes the VOLTAGE across the VARIABLE RESISTOR to
DECREASE ...

② ... until the NOT GATE recognises this input to be LOW (or OFF)
in which case the gate inverts it to a HIGH (or ON) which
causes a current to flow ...

③ ... into the TRANSISTOR via a RESISTOR which reduces the
amount of current flowing (in order to prevent damage to
the transistor). The transistor simply acts as a SWITCH ...

④ ... allowing a small current to flow into the RELAY which
switches on the larger current needed for the OUTPUT DEVICE
eg. a lamp. Across the relay is a reverse biased DIODE which
protects the transistor by acting as a buffer when the relay is
switched off.

ADVANTAGES AND DISADVANTAGES OF USING ELECTRONIC SYSTEMS

CCTV ...	MOBILE PHONES ...	INTERNET ...
Benefits of SECURITY against theft and vandalism.	Benefits for WORKING PRACTICES.	Benefits of its EDUCATIONAL VALUE.
Drawback in its potential for the invasion of PRIVACY.	Drawback in their potential for INTRUSION and HEALTH HAZARDS.	Drawback of allowing UNSUITABLE MATERIAL to be transmitted to children.

CAPACITORS

CAPACITORS
A CAPACITOR is a CHARGE STORER. If a current 'flows into' an
uncharged capacitor, charge is stored on the capacitor and the
voltage or potential difference (p.d.) across the capacitor increases.

symbol for a capacitor

p.d. or voltage now across capacitor

CHARGING AND DISCHARGING CAPACITORS
The GREATER the RESISTANCE of the charging or discharging
circuit and the GREATER the value of the CAPACITOR, the LONGER
it takes for the CAPACITOR to CHARGE or DISCHARGE.

If we CHARGE a capacitor ...

NORMAL | GREATER RESISTANCE | GREATER VALUE OF CAPACITOR
Time | Time | Time
 | TAKES LONGER | TAKES LONGER

If we DISCHARGE a capacitor ...

NORMAL | GREATER RESISTANCE | GREATER VALUE OF CAPACITOR
Time | Time | Time
 | TAKES LONGER | TAKES LONGER

Capacitors can be used as a TIMER in an electronic system.

CAPACITOR AS A TIME DELAY SWITCH

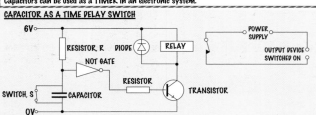

6V | RESISTOR, R | DIODE | RELAY | POWER SUPPLY | OUTPUT DEVICE SWITCHED ON
NOT GATE | RESISTOR
SWITCH, S | CAPACITOR | TRANSISTOR
0V

LENSES AND RAY DIAGRAMS

CONVERGING AND DIVERGING LENSES
A CONVERGING (or convex) lens is thickest at its centre while a DIVERGING (or concave) lens is
thinnest at its centre. Due to this difference in curvature, PARALLEL RAYS of light pass differently
through them.

A CONVERGING LENS ...

Parallel rays of light | F

A DIVERGING LENS ...

Parallel rays of light | F

The image formed is nearly always REAL | The image formed is always VIRTUAL

• A CAMERA uses a CONVERGING LENS. The image formed is smaller than the object and
is nearer to the lens compared to the object.

RAY DIAGRAMS
To construct a ray diagram TWO rays of light need to be drawn from the top of the object.

①. OBJECT | F | AXIS

②. OBJECT | F | AXIS

TWO EXAMPLES

OBJECT | ZF | F | 2F | AXIS | IMAGE

IMAGE | OBJECT | 2F | F | 2F

• The position of the object beyond 2F is the arrangement used in cameras
• The position of the object between F and LENS is the arrangement used in magnifying glasses.

1. Look at the diagram of a relay below and choose words from the list to complete the following sentences.

A. CONTACTS.
B. LARGER CURRENT.
C. SMALL CURRENT.
D. ELECTROMAGNET.

PIVOT
IRON ARMATURE
CONTACTS
ELECTROMAGNET (with iron core)

A __1__ flows through the coil of the relay and switches on the __2__ . This causes the __3__ to close which switches on a __4__ .

2. Match the words below with each of the numbered diagrams.

A. THERMISTOR.
B. LIGHT DEPENDENT RESISTOR.
C. LIGHT EMITTING DIODE.
D. BUZZER.

3. Which two of the following statements about light emitting diodes are correct?

A. They give out light when the current flows in one particular direction only.
B. They give out light when the current flows in either direction.
C. They give out light as soon as they are switched on.
D. They don't give out light when the current flows in the 'wrong' direction.
E. They detect changes in light intensity.

4. Electronic systems rely on processors. Examples of these are logic gates.

4.1 Which one of the following statements is true of an 'AND' gate?
A. The output is 1, only if the first and second inputs are 1.
B. The output is 1, if the first or second inputs are 1.
C. The output is 1, if the input is 0.
D. The output is 1, only if the first and second inputs are 0.

4.2 Which one of the following statements is true of an 'OR' gate?
A. The output is 1, if the first and second inputs are 1.
B. The output is 1, if the first or second inputs are 1.
C. The output is 1, if the input is 0.
D. The output is 1, only if the first and second inputs are 0.

4.3 Which one of the following statements is true of a 'NOT' gate?
A. The output is 1, only if the first and second inputs are 1.
B. The output is 1, if the first or second inputs are 1.
C. The output is 1, if the input is 0.
D. The output is 1, only if the first and second inputs are 0.

4.4 Which logic gates could be used to give the following truth table information:
First input 1, Second input 1, output 1?
A. AND, OR and NOT.
B. OR and NOT.
C. AND and NOT.
D. AND and OR.

5. The questions below refer to this diagram of a potential divider circuit:

V_{in} = 6V, R_1, R_2, V_{out}, 0V

5.1 If $R_1 = 10\Omega$ and $R_2 = 5\Omega$, what would the output voltage be?
A. 4 volts.
B. 15 volts.
C. 2 volts.
D. 3 volts.

5.2 If $R_1 = 5\Omega$ and $R_2 = 5\Omega$, what would the output voltage be?
A. 6 volts.
B. 10 volts.
C. 2 volts.
D. 3 volts.

5.3 If $R_1 = 5\Omega$ and $R_2 = 1\Omega$, what would the output voltage be?
A. 1 volt.
B. 5 volts.
C. 30 volts.
D. 1.2 volts.

5.4 If $R_1 = 15\Omega$ and $R_2 = 30\Omega$, what would the output voltage be?
A. 12 volts.
B. 4 volts.
C. 2 volts.
D. 3 volts.

6. This question relates to converging and diverging lenses.

6.1 Which of the following best describes a converging lens?
A. Thinnest at its centre and the image is always virtual.
B. Thickest at its centre and the image is nearly always real.
C. Thickest at its centre and the image is nearly always virtual.
D. Light is refracted outwards by the lens.

6.2 Which of the following best describes a diverging lens?
A. Thinnest at its centre and the image is always virtual.
B. Thickest at its centre and the image is nearly always real.
C. Thickest at its centre and the image is nearly always virtual.
D. Light is refracted inwards.

6.3 What is the focus of a lens?
A. The point to which rays are refracted.
B. The point from which rays appear to be refracted.
C. The point to which certain rays are refracted as from which certain rays appear to be refracted.
D. The point where all the light is focused.

6.4 Which one of the following statements best describes the image formed by a camera?
A. The image is larger than the object and nearer to the lens.
B. The image is smaller than the object and nearer to the lens.
C. The image is larger than the object and further from the lens.
D. The image is smaller than the object and further from the lens.

7. Ray diagrams can be drawn to show the formation of an image by a converging lens.

2F   F   F   2F

7.1 When the object is beyond 2F, the image is …
A. Real, right way up and bigger.
B. Real, right way up and smaller.
C. Real, upside down and bigger.
D. Real, upside down and smaller.

7.2 When the object is at 2F, the image is …
A. Real, upside down and smaller.
B. Real, upside down and the same size as the object.
C. Real, upside down and bigger.
D. Real, the right way up and the same size as the object.

7.3 When the object is between 2F and F, the image is …
A. Real, upside down and smaller.
B. Real, the right way up and smaller.
C. Real, the right way up and bigger.
D. Real, upside down and bigger.

7.4 When the object is between F and the lens, the image is …
A. Virtual, the right way up and bigger.
B. Virtual, upside down and bigger.
C. Virtual, upside down and smaller.
D. Virtual, the right way up and smaller.

Louis Pasteur 1822-1895

Pasteur was a French scientist who discovered the reason why food eventually goes bad. He realised that there are microorganisms in the air which can get into foods, multiply, and make the food go bad. He performed the following experiment to provide evidence for his theories:

A solution containing nutrients was poured into a flask.

The neck of the flask was melted and pulled as above.

The nutrient solution was boiled to kill microbes and drive out air.

The nutrient solution was left for several weeks without showing signs of decay.

When the neck was snapped off in a similar experiment the nutrient solution started to decay in days.

The microbes causing the decay of exposed foods are mainly BACTERIA and MOULDS. These and other microorganisms can also cause disease and when they do so they are called PATHOGENS.

Treatment Of Disease

The symptoms of disease are often controlled by using PAINKILLERS. You will be familiar with the mild versions of these we use at home eg. aspirin. However, although painkillers are very useful, they do not kill the pathogens. ANTIBIOTICS are often used against bacteria. Perhaps the most commonly known antibiotic is penicillin. These help to cure bacterial diseases by killing infective bacteria inside the body, however they cannot be used to kill VIRUSES which live and reproduce inside cells! It is difficult to develop drugs which kill viruses without also damaging the body's tissues.

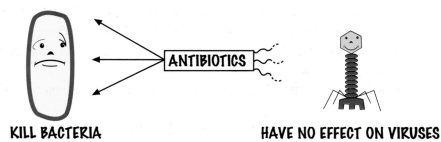

KILL BACTERIA   HAVE NO EFFECT ON VIRUSES

Over-use Of Antibiotics

Many strains of bacteria have developed resistance to antibiotics as a result of NATURAL SELECTION. In other words some individual bacteria in a particular strain have natural resistance. In the event of the majority of the strain being wiped out by antibiotics this leaves the field clear for the resistant bacteria to multiply quickly, passing on their resistance. It is therefore necessary to have a range of different antibiotics and to select the one that is most effective for treatment of a particular infection.

Development of further resistance is avoided by preventing over-use of antibiotics.

Active Immunity

People can be immunised against a disease by introducing small quantities of dead or inactive forms of the pathogen into the body. This is usually achieved through vaccination.

The external protein structure of the pathogen contained within the vaccine is recognised as an ANTIGEN ('foreign body') and stimulates the white cells to produce ANTIBODIES which react with and destroy the antigens (and therefore the pathogens).

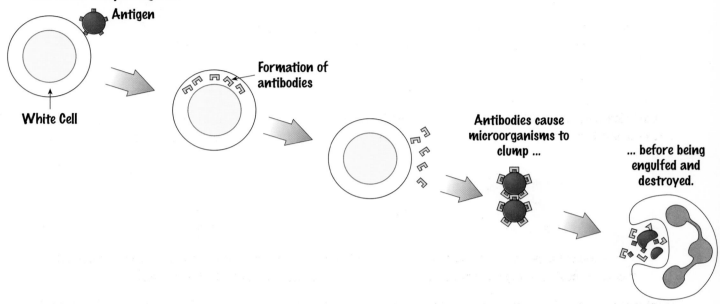

Antigen

White Cell

Formation of antibodies

Antibodies cause microorganisms to clump ...

... before being engulfed and destroyed.

This type of vaccination gives a person IMMUNITY to future infections by the pathogen because the white cells 'remember' how to make the appropriate antibody and so respond very quickly, in much the same way as if the person had had the disease previously. This is called ACTIVE IMMUNITY.

Effectiveness Against Viral Pathogens

Vaccination can be used most effectively to protect against viral pathogens and forms a vital part of the overall health strategy since these pathogens are resistant to antibiotics. A classic case is the MMR vaccine which is used to protect children against measles, mumps and rubella, none of which will respond to antibiotics.

Passive Immunity

In instances where a person has been exposed to a dangerous pathogen to which they have not been previously immunised, it is necessary to boost their own response to the pathogen by injecting ready-made antibodies directly into the bloodstream. This is called PASSIVE IMMUNITY, an example being the use of rabies antibodies after a person has been bitten by a potentially rabid dog.

These antibodies obviously have to be already in stock, and they are produced commercially by pharmaceutical companies.

Remember, the key differences between active and passive 'immunity':

ACTIVE IMMUNITY	PASSIVE IMMUNITY
The immune system is 'primed' for future infections by introducing a mild form of the pathogen. The white cells 'remember' how to produce the appropriate antibodies and so can respond quickly to the infection.	When a person has already been exposed to a new pathogen, it may take too long for his white cells to respond. Ready-made antibodies are injected to provide immediate protection.

T Cells And B Cells

The T cells and B cells are two particular types of white blood cell which form the key components of the immune response.

- T cells have special receptors on their surface membrane which can recognise and attach to a particular antigen. The T cells can then destroy cells which have this antigen.

RECEPTOR SITES ON T CELLS

ANTIGENS ON SURFACE MEMBRANE OF 'FOREIGN' CELL (PATHOGEN)

RECEPTORS ON T CELLS ATTACH TO ANTIGENS ON PATHOGEN AND DESTROY THEM

- B cells, when stimulated by T cells, can multiply quickly to form clones. These clones then secrete antibodies which are specific to a particular antigen.

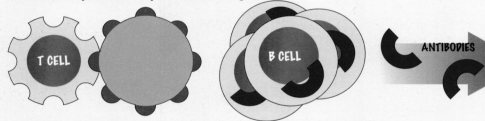

T CELLS DETECT AND ATTACH TO ANTIGEN ON 'FOREIGN' CELL

T CELLS STIMULATE B CELLS TO MULTIPLY AND SECRETE ANTIBODIES

ANTIBODIES ATTACH TO SPECIFIC ANTIGENS AND DESTROY THEM

The Immune Response

The body effectively launches a two-pronged attack on the 'invader' using T and B cells ...

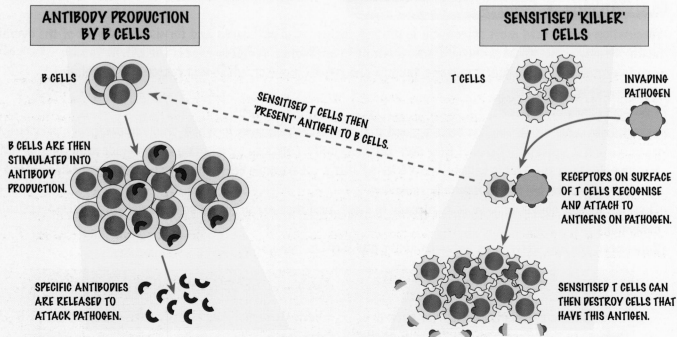

ANTIBODY PRODUCTION BY B CELLS

B CELLS

SENSITISED T CELLS THEN 'PRESENT' ANTIGEN TO B CELLS.

B CELLS ARE THEN STIMULATED INTO ANTIBODY PRODUCTION.

SPECIFIC ANTIBODIES ARE RELEASED TO ATTACK PATHOGEN.

SENSITISED 'KILLER' T CELLS

T CELLS

INVADING PATHOGEN

RECEPTORS ON SURFACE OF T CELLS RECOGNISE AND ATTACH TO ANTIGENS ON PATHOGEN.

SENSITISED T CELLS CAN THEN DESTROY CELLS THAT HAVE THIS ANTIGEN.

Some T cells and B cells retain the ability to respond to this antigen and are referred to as 'memory cells'. These remain in the body and ensure that antibody production takes place very quickly if the same antigen enters the body for a second time. This 'immunological memory' provides immunity following both a natural infection and after vaccination.

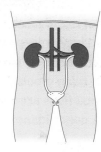

The Function Of The Kidney

In the majority of humans there are two kidneys situated on the back wall of the abdomen. Their function is to maintain the concentrations of dissolved substances in the blood, and also to remove all UREA. If the kidneys fail then there is no way of removing excess substances. This will ultimately result in death.

Using A Dialysis Machine

In a dialysis machine, a person's blood flows between partially permeable membranes. These membranes are made from a material which is similar to the Visking tubing you may have used in experiments on osmosis.

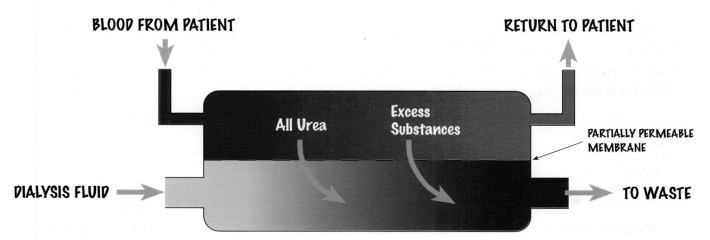

As the blood flows through the machine, it is separated from the dialysis fluid only by the partially permeable membranes. These membranes allow all the urea, and any excess substances to pass from the blood to the dialysis fluid. This restores the concentrations of dissolved substances in the blood to their normal levels.
However, dialysis must be carried out at regular intervals in order to maintain the patient's health.

Dialysis In More Detail

Dialysis depends on the movement of substances across the partially-permeable membrane within the dialysis machine. This membrane won't allow large molecules to pass through it - let alone the actual red and white blood cells! However, smaller molecules such as water, ions and urea are free to pass through the membrane <u>in either direction</u>.
To ensure that these molecules move in the direction we want and that we don't lose substances such as glucose and some ions, we have to carefully control the concentration of substances within the dialysis fluid. If the concentration of a substance is the same in both the blood and the fluid then there will be no net movement. Consequently the dialysis fluid contains the ideal concentrations of ions, water and glucose that the patient should have in his plasma. If the patient's concentrations are higher (as they almost certainly will be) then those substances which are in excess, will diffuse across the partially permeable membrane.

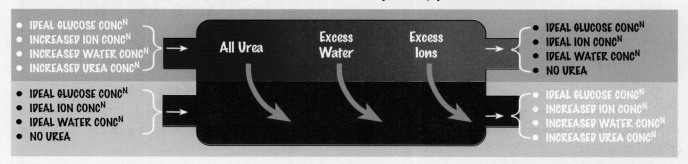

Kidney Transplants

A kidney transplant enables a diseased kidney to be replaced by a healthy one from a donor. This is performed in the event of <u>both</u> kidneys failing - one is quite sufficient to do a perfectly good job.

The main problem with kidney transplants is the possibility of REJECTION by the immune system. The following precautions are taken to minimise the risk of this ...

- A donor kidney with a 'tissue type' as close as possible to that of the recipient is used. In other words it must carry similar antigens. This is best achieved if the donor is a very close relative.
- The bone marrow of the recipient is irradiated to stop the production of white cells. This reduces the likelihood of rejection in the early stages after transplantation.
- The recipient is treated with drugs which suppress the immune response. Again, this lessens the chances of rejection in the early stages.
- The recipient is kept in sterile conditions for some time after the operation to lessen the risk of infection due to his suppressed immune system.

	DIALYSIS	KIDNEY TRANSPLANT
ADVANTAGES	• No rejection can occur. • More readily available and can be used by patients waiting for a transplant.	• No need for regular dialysis - can lead less restricted life. • Nearly 80% success rate if tissue types match.
DISADVANTAGES	• Regular sessions in hospital or at home on dialysis machine (10 hours). • Diet has to be controlled - some foods can only be eaten when the person is connected to the dialysis machine.	• Rejection can occur where body's defence system 'attacks' the kidney. • Anti-rejection drugs may need to be taken for the rest of the patient's life.

Blood Matching During Transplantation

During the course of the operation, a blood transfusion may be required. The blood used must be matched with the blood group of the recipient to prevent agglutination (clumping of the red cells).

In the ABO system of blood grouping, there are ANTIGENS on the surface of the red blood cells and ANTIBODIES in the blood plasma.

BLOOD TYPE A	• Blood cells contain type A antigens. • Plasma contains anti b antibodies.
BLOOD TYPE B	• Blood cells contain type B antigens. • Plasma contains anti a antibodies.
BLOOD TYPE AB	• Blood cells contain both A and B antigens. • Plasma contains NO antibodies.
BLOOD TYPE O	• Blood cells contain NO antigens. • Plasma contains both anti a and anti b antibodies.

COMPATIBILITY TABLE

RECIPIENT

BLOOD TYPE	A b	B a	AB —	O ab
A b	✔	✗	✔	✗
B a	✗	✔	✔	✗
AB _	✗	✗	✔	✗
O ab	✔	✔	✔	✔

DONOR

UPPERCASE = ANTIGENS

lowercase = antibodies

- The key to understanding whether or not a particular transfusion will be compatible with the patient's blood relies on the following ...

'The recipient's plasma must not contain antibodies which would act against the antigens on the donor's red blood cells.'

You should be familiar with the structure of the following microorganisms.

VIRUSES

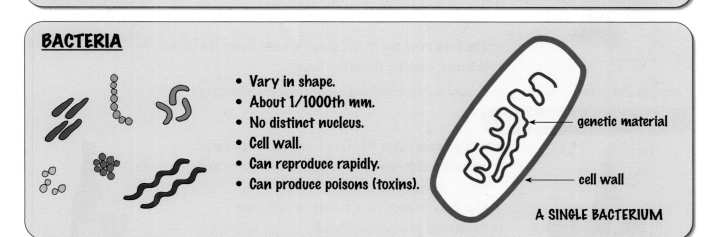

genes
protein coat

- Vary in shape.
- About 1/10,000th mm.
- Consist of protein coat surrounding a few genes.
- On borderline between living and non-living.
- Live and reproduce inside living cells.

injects genes ...
... makes copies ...
... burst out

BACTERIA

- Vary in shape.
- About 1/1000th mm.
- No distinct nucleus.
- Cell wall.
- Can reproduce rapidly.
- Can produce poisons (toxins).

genetic material

cell wall

A SINGLE BACTERIUM

FUNGI

There are two types of fungi which you need to know about ...

i) MOULDS

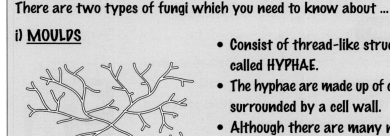

- Consist of thread-like structures called HYPHAE.
- The hyphae are made up of cytoplasm surrounded by a cell wall.
- Although there are many nuclei present in the hyphae, there are no distinct cells.
- They reproduce asexually by producing structures containing spores.

BRANCHING NETWORK OF HYPHAE

spores

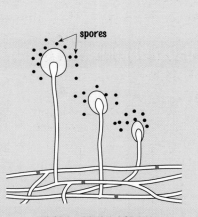

BREAD MOULD SPORES

ii) YEAST

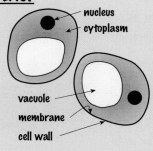

nucleus
cytoplasm

vacuole
membrane
cell wall

- Yeast is a single-celled organism.
- Each cell has a nucleus, cytoplasm and a membrane surrounded by a cell wall.
- Yeast reproduces by 'budding'.

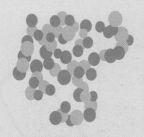

YEAST 'BUDDING'

How Yeast Works

Yeast can respire without oxygen (anaerobic respiration) to produce carbon dioxide and ethanol (alcohol).

GLUCOSE ⟶ ETHANOL + CARBON DIOXIDE + ENERGY

This is called **FERMENTATION** and has many industrial applications (see below).

Yeast can also respire using oxygen (aerobic respiration) to produce carbon dioxide and water.

GLUCOSE + OXYGEN ⟶ WATER + CARBON DIOXIDE + ENERGY

Aerobic respiration produces more energy and is necessary for the yeast to grow and reproduce.

Using Yeast In Baking

- A mixture of yeast and sugar is added to flour.
- The mixture is left in a warm place.
- The carbon dioxide from the respiring yeast makes the dough rise.
- The bubbles of gas in the dough expand when the bread is baked, making the bread 'light'.

Also, as the bread is baked, any alcohol produced during respiration evaporates off.

Using Yeast In Brewing

- In a process called **MALTING**, the starch in barley grains is broken down into a sugary solution by enzymes in the germinating grains.
- This sugary solution is extracted and then fermented to produce alcohol.
- Hops are then added to give the beer flavour.
- In wine-making the yeast uses the natural sugars in the grapes as its energy source.

Using Bacteria In Yoghurt Production

FERMENTER

- In the production of yoghurt, a starter culture of bacteria is added to warm milk in a fermenting vessel.
- The bacteria ferment the milk sugar (lactose) producing lactic acid which provides a sour taste.
- The lactic acid causes the milk to clot and solidify into yoghurt.

Using Bacteria And Moulds In Cheese Production

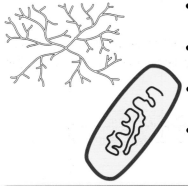

- In the production of cheese, a starter culture of bacteria (different from the one above) is added to warm milk.
- Curds are produced which have a more solid consistency than yoghurt.
- The curds are separated from the rest of the liquid (whey).
- Bacteria and moulds are added to the solid curds to cause the cheese to slowly ripen. They may also be used to provide the 'veining' in blue cheeses.

Antibiotic Production

Microorganisms can be grown in large vessels called **FERMENTERS** (see diagram below) and used to produce useful products such as antibiotics.

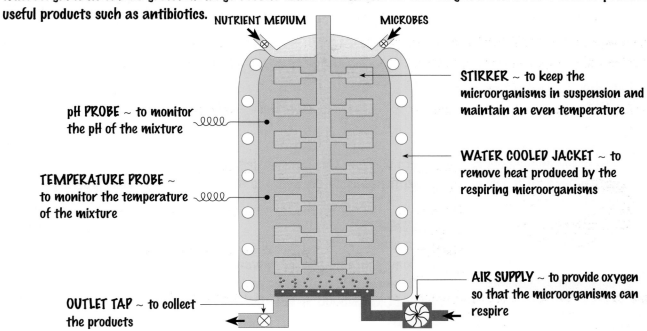

NUTRIENT MEDIUM

MICROBES

STIRRER ~ to keep the microorganisms in suspension and maintain an even temperature

pH PROBE ~ to monitor the pH of the mixture

WATER COOLED JACKET ~ to remove heat produced by the respiring microorganisms

TEMPERATURE PROBE ~ to monitor the temperature of the mixture

AIR SUPPLY ~ to provide oxygen so that the microorganisms can respire

OUTLET TAP ~ to collect the products

The antibiotic **PENICILLIN** is made by growing the mould, Penicillium, in a fermenter such as the one above. The medium contains sugar and other nutrients which tend to be used up for growth before the mould starts to make **PENICILLIN**.

Fuel Production

Fuels can be made from natural products via fermentation. Unlike the process above however, <u>all oxygen must be excluded so that **ANAEROBIC** fermentation can occur.</u>
Biogas, which is mainly methane, can be produced in this way using a wide range of organic or waste material which contains carbohydrates.

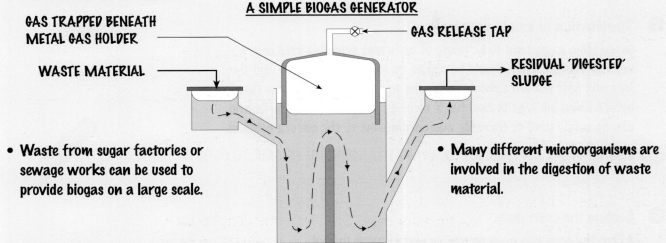

A SIMPLE BIOGAS GENERATOR

GAS TRAPPED BENEATH METAL GAS HOLDER

GAS RELEASE TAP

WASTE MATERIAL

RESIDUAL 'DIGESTED' SLUDGE

• Waste from sugar factories or sewage works can be used to provide biogas on a large scale.

• Many different microorganisms are involved in the digestion of waste material.

Anaerobic respiration can also be used to produce **ETHANOL-BASED FUELS**, from sugar cane juices or glucose derived from maize starch by the action of carbohydrase. The ethanol produced needs to be distilled from the other products of fermentation, and can then be used in motor vehicles.

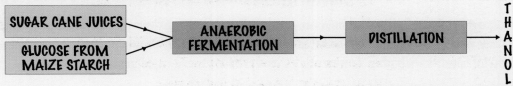

SUGAR CANE JUICES

GLUCOSE FROM MAIZE STARCH

ANAEROBIC FERMENTATION

DISTILLATION

E
T
H
A
N
O
L

Preparing A Culture Medium

Microorganisms are grown in a culture medium containing various nutrients which the particular microorganism may need. These nutrients may include ...

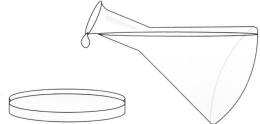

- CARBOHYDRATES - as an energy resource
- MINERAL IONS
- VITAMINS
- PROTEINS

Agar is most commonly used as the growth medium. This is a soft, jelly-like substance which melts easily and re-solidifies around 50°C. The nutrients mentioned above are added to the agar to provide ideal growing conditions for cultures.

Preparing Uncontaminated Cultures

If the cultures we want to investigate become contaminated by unwanted microorganisms, it is possible that these 'rogue' microorganisms may produce undesirable substances which may prove harmful.
THEREFORE IT IS ONLY SAFE TO USE MICROORGANISMS IF WE HAVE A PURE CULTURE CONTAINING ONE PARTICULAR SPECIES OF MICROORGANISM.

In order to prepare useful products, uncontaminated cultures of microorganisms are prepared using the following procedures:

❶ Sterilisation of petri dishes and culture medium

Both petri dishes and culture medium must be sterilised using an autoclave. This is basically a pressure cooker which exposes the dishes and the agar to HIGH TEMPERATURE and HIGH PRESSURE to kill off any unwanted microorganisms.

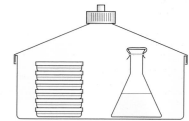

❷ Sterilisation of inoculating loops

Inoculating loops tend to be made of nichrome wire inserted into a wooden handle. They should be picked up as if holding a pen and the loop and half the wire should be heated to red heat in a bunsen flame, before being allowed to cool for 5 seconds. They are then sterile and can be safely used to transfer microorganisms to the culture medium.

🅝🅑 DO NOT BLOW ON THE LOOP OR WAVE IT AROUND IN THE AIR TO COOL IT!

❸ Sealing the petri dish

After the agar has been poured in and allowed to cool, the petri dish should be sealed with tape to prevent entry of microorganisms and clearly labelled on the base before being stored upside down so that condensation forms in the lid.

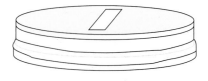

🅝🅑 In schools and colleges cultures should only be incubated at a maximum of 25°C to prevent the growth of seriously nasty pathogens that grow at body temperature (37°C) and potentially are harmful to humans. In industrial conditions higher temperatures can produce more rapid growth.

CONTROLLING DISEASE

<u>LOUIS PASTEUR</u> performed a classical experiment to show that food goes bad because of microorganisms in the air. Most often these microorganisms are BACTERIA and MOULDS. When they cause disease they are called PATHOGENS.

TREATMENT OF DISEASE

- PAINKILLERS control the symptoms of disease only.
- ANTIBIOTICS are used to kill bacteria but can't kill viruses.
  However, some bacteria have developed resistance to antibiotics as a result of natural selection.
- Therefore it is important to avoid over-use of antibiotics.
- Since viruses live and reproduce inside living cells, it is difficult to develop drugs which kill them without damaging the body's cells.

ACTIVE IMMUNITY

Dead or inactive pathogen is injected. Protein-based ANTIGENS stimulate the white cells to form antibodies, to destroy the antigens.

- Used particularly against viral pathogens such as measles and mumps.

<u>PASSIVE IMMUNITY</u> occurs when antibodies have to be injected directly to give immediate protection against a pathogen eg. rabies vaccine.

THE IMMUNE RESPONSE

- T cells attach to antigens and destroy them. B cells are stimulated by T cells to produce clones which secrete the appropriate antibodies.

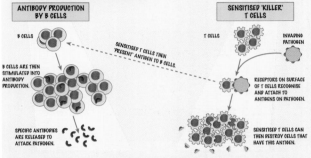

'Immunological memory' due to T and B cells provides immunity after both natural infection and vaccination.

KIDNEY FAILURE

DIALYSIS

- A partially permeable membrane separates the blood and the dialysis fluid. Urea is removed and the concentrations of dissolved substances are restored to normal levels.

To prevent useful substances being lost, the concentrations of glucose and mineral ions in the dialysis fluid is kept at the level ideal for a healthy human. Only wastes and substances in excess will then diffuse across into the fluid.

KIDNEY TRANSPLANTS

Precautions must be taken to minimise the risk of REJECTION.

- A donor kidney with a similar 'tissue type' must be used.
- The bone marrow of the recipient is irradiated to reduce white cell production in order to minimise the chance of an immune response.
- The recipient is treated with drugs to suppress the immune response.
- The recipient is kept in sterile conditions to lessen the chance of infection.

	DIALYSIS	TRANSPLANT
ADVANTAGES	• No rejection • Greater availability	• No dialysis needed • 80% success rate
DISADVANTAGES	• 10 hour sessions • Diet must be controlled	• Rejection can occur • Anti-rejection drugs needed

BLOOD MATCHING

- In the ABO system there are antigens on the surface of the red blood cells and ...
- ... antibodies in the plasma. The compatibility table opposite shows the possible acceptable combinations.

COMPATIBILITY TABLE

		RECIPIENT			
BLOOD TYPE		A b	B a	AB __	O ab
DONOR	A b	✓	✗	✓	✗
	B a	✗	✓	✓	✗
	AB __	✗	✗	✓	✗
	O ab	✓	✓	✓	✓

UPPERCASE = ANTIGENS
LOWERCASE = ANTIBODIES

MICROORGANISMS AND THEIR SAFE USE

VIRUSES

- Vary in shape.
- About 1/10,000th mm.
- Consists of protein coat surrounding a few genes.
- On borderline between living and non-living.

genes, protein coat

injects genes ... ... makes copies ... ... burst out

BACTERIA

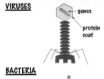

- Vary in shape.
- About 1/1000th mm.
- No distinct nucleus.
- Cell wall.
- Can reproduce rapidly.
- Can produce poisons (toxins).

A SINGLE BACTERIUM

genetic material, cell wall

FUNGI

There are two types of fungi which you need to know about ...

I) MOULDS

BRANCHING NETWORK OF HYPHAE

- Consist of thread-like structures called HYPHAE.
- The hyphae are made up of cytoplasm surrounded by a cell wall.
- Although there are many nuclei present in the hyphae, there are no distinct cells.
- They reproduce asexually by producing structures containing spores.

BREAD MOULD SPORES

II) YEAST

NUCLEUS, CYTOPLASM, VACUOLE, MEMBRANE, CELL WALL

- Yeast is a single-celled organism.
- Each cell has a nucleus, cytoplasm and a membrane surrounded by a cell wall.
- Yeast reproduces by 'budding'.

YEAST 'BUDDING'

PREPARING UNCONTAMINATED CULTURES

A culture medium would usually contain the following nutrients:

- CARBOHYDRATES • MINERAL IONS • VITAMINS • PROTEINS in an agar medium.

For the culture to be uncontaminated (ie. containing only the microbe you want to cultivate) the following should be observed:

1. STERILISE PETRI DISHES AND CULTURE MEDIUM in an autoclave at high temperature and pressure.
2. STERILISE INOCULATING LOOPS by heating to red heat in a bunsen flame before allowing to cool for 5 seconds.
3. SEAL THE PETRI DISH after preparation with tape to prevent entry of microbes. Clearly label it on the base and store upside down so that condensation forms on the base. INCUBATE ONLY AT A MAXIMUM OF 25°C!!!

USES OF MICROORGANISMS IN INDUSTRY

HOW YEAST WORKS

1) ANAEROBICALLY: GLUCOSE ⟶ ETHANOL + CARBON DIOXIDE + ENERGY
2) AEROBICALLY: GLUCOSE ⟶ WATER + CARBON DIOXIDE + ENERGY

Aerobic respiration produces more energy and is necessary for growth.

<u>YEAST IN BAKING</u> Yeast and sugar are added to flour and left at a warm temperature. CO_2 produced by the yeast makes the dough rise, and these bubbles of gas make the bread light when baked.

<u>YEAST IN BREWING</u> Starch in barley grains is broken down into a sugary solution (MALTING) by enzymes. This solution is then fermented to produce alcohol. In wine making the yeast uses natural sugars.

<u>BACTERIA IN YOGHURT PRODUCTION</u> A starter culture of bacteria is added to warm milk and ferments the milk sugar (lactose) to lactic acid, which causes the milk to clot and solidify into yoghurt.

<u>BACTERIA AND MOULDS IN CHEESE PRODUCTION</u> A different starter culture is added to warm milk and produces curds. These are separated from the whey (liquid) and other bacteria and moulds are added to cause it to ripen in particular ways.

<u>ANTIBIOTIC PRODUCTION</u> takes place in a FERMENTER (AEROBICALLY).

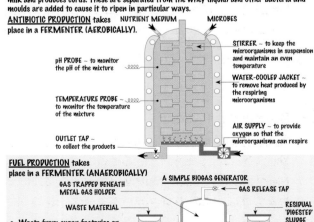

NUTRIENT MEDIUM, MICROBES

STIRRER – to keep the microorganisms in suspension and maintain an even temperature

pH PROBE – to monitor the pH of the mixture

WATER-COOLED JACKET – to remove heat produced by the respiring microorganisms

TEMPERATURE PROBE – to monitor the temperature of the mixture

AIR SUPPLY – to provide oxygen so that the microorganisms can respire

OUTLET TAP – to collect the products

<u>FUEL PRODUCTION</u> takes place in a FERMENTER (ANAEROBICALLY)

A SIMPLE BIOGAS GENERATOR

GAS TRAPPED BENEATH METAL GAS HOLDER

GAS RELEASE TAP

WASTE MATERIAL

RESIDUAL 'DIGESTED' SLUDGE

- Waste from sugar factories or sewage works can be used to provide biogas on a large scale.
- Sugar cane juices or glucose can be ANAEROBICALLY fermented into ethanol-based fuels.

1.
  a) What reason did Louis Pasteur provide for food eventually going bad?

  b) To provide evidence for his theories a solution containing nutrients was poured into a flask which was then boiled as shown in the diagram. What was the purpose of boiling the solution?

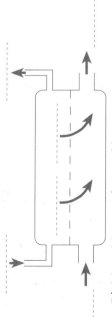

  c) The nutrient solution was then left for several weeks. What did Pasteur observe? What did Pasteur observe?

  d) In a similar experiment the neck of the flask was snapped off. What did Pasteur observe?

  e) Give as many reasons as possible why this was a fair test.

2. What are pathogens?

3.
  a) Give one advantage and one disadvantage in using painkillers.

  b) Give one advantage and one disadvantage in using antibiotics.

4.
  a) Why have some strains of bacteria developed resistance to antibiotics?

  b) Why is it important to have a range of different antibiotics for the treatment of a particular infection?

5.
  a) Explain using diagrams how a person can be immunised against a disease by introducing small quantities of dead or inactive forms of the pathogen into the body.

  b) Why does this type of vaccination give a person immunity to future infections by the pathogen?

  c) Vaccination can also be used to protect a person against viral pathogens. Explain why this form of immunisation is very important.

6.
  a) What is the difference between active immunity and passive immunity?

  b) Give an example where a person would be immunised actively against a disease.

  c) Give an example where a person would be immunised passively against a disease.

7.
  a) What are T cells and B cells?

  b) Explain, using diagrams, how T cells destroy cells with a particular antigen.

  c) Explain, using diagrams, how B cells destroy cells with a particular antigen.

8.
  a) Antigens are destroyed when the body effectively launches a two-pronged attack using T and B cells. Explain, using diagrams, how this happens.

  b) Why are some T cells and B cells referred to as 'memory cells'?

9.
  a) What are the functions of the kidneys?

  b) The diagram below shows a simple dialysis machine. Label it using the following:
EXCESS SUBSTANCES, BLOOD FROM PATIENT, TO WASTE, ALL UREA, RETURN TO PATIENT, DIALYSIS FLUID

  c) Why must dialysis be carried out at regular intervals?

10.
  a) Why is it essential to control the concentration of substances within the dialysis fluid?

  b) If a person's blood has a higher than normal concentration of urea what would be the effect of the dialysis machine?

  c) If a person's blood has a lower than normal concentration of glucose what would be the effect of the dialysis machine?

11.
  a) What is the main problem with a person having a kidney transplant?

  b) Give four ways of minimising the effect of this problem.

  c) Give two advantages and two disadvantages for a person receiving dialysis rather than a kidney transplant.

12.
  a) During the course of a kidney transplant operation a blood transfusion may be required. Why must the blood used match the blood group of the recipient?

  b) Copy and complete the compatibility table using a ✔ for a successful transfusion, and a ✗ for an unsuccessful one

	RECIPIENT			
	A b	B a	AB –	O ab
DONOR				
A b				
B a				
AB				
O ab				

UPPERCASE = ANTIGENS, LOWERCASE = ANTIBODIES

  c) What criteria must exist between the recipient's plasma and the donor's red blood cells for a compatible transfusion?

13.
  a) Match the characteristics to bacteria and viruses. One has been done for you.

Bacteria   **Viruses**

- About $\frac{1}{1,000}$ th mm
- Has a protein coat
- Vary in shape
- No distinct nucleus
- Killed by antibiotics
- About $\frac{1}{10,000}$ th mm

  b) Match the characteristics to moulds and yeast.

Moulds   **Yeast**

- Reproduce by 'budding'
- Consist of thread-like structures
- Single-celled organism
- Reproduce asexually
- Have no distinct cells

14.
  a) What is the difference between anaerobic respiration and aerobic respiration?

  b) What part does yeast play in baking?

  c) What part does yeast play in brewing?

  d) What part do bacteria play in the production of yoghurt?

  e) What part do bacteria and moulds play in the production of cheese?

15.
  a) Label the diagram of the fermenter.

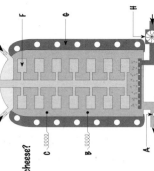

  b) What is the name of the mould used to make penicillin?

  c) Explain, using a diagram, how biogas can be produced.

  d) Explain how ethanol-based fuels can be produced.

16.
  a) Name four different nutrients that a culture medium may contain in order for microorganisms to grow.

  b) What is agar?

  c) What disadvantage is there in having unwanted microorganisms in the culture which is being investigated?

  d) Explain what procedures would need to be carried out in order to produce uncontaminated cultures of microorganisms.

Sulphuric Acid And Its Uses

SULPHURIC ACID is a very important chemical with many uses. Even the industrial development of a country can be measured by the amount of sulphuric acid they use every year. It can be used ...

... as the acid in
CAR BATTERIES

... to make
DETERGENTS

... to make
FERTILISERS

Manufacture Of Sulphuric Acid

SULPHURIC ACID is manufactured using three raw materials: SULPHUR, AIR and WATER.
There are FOUR STEPS in its manufacture ...

1 SULPHUR → BURNT IN AIR → SULPHUR DIOXIDE

- SULPHUR is burnt in AIR to form SULPHUR DIOXIDE.

$$SULPHUR + OXYGEN \longrightarrow SULPHUR\ DIOXIDE : S_{(s)} + O_{2(g)} \longrightarrow SO_{2(g)}$$

2 SULPHUR DIOXIDE → MORE AIR AND V_2O_5 → SULPHUR TRIOXIDE

- The SULPHUR DIOXIDE is then mixed with more AIR and the mixture is passed over ...
... a CATALYST of VANADIUM OXIDE, V_2O_5, at a TEMPERATURE of about 450°C ...
... and a PRESSURE of between ONE and TWO ATMOSPHERES to form SULPHUR TRIOXIDE.

$$SULPHUR\ DIOXIDE + OXYGEN \rightleftharpoons SULPHUR\ TRIOXIDE : 2SO_{2(g)} + O_{2(g)} \rightleftharpoons 2SO_{3(g)}$$

3 SULPHUR TRIOXIDE → DISSOLVED IN CONC^N. H_2SO_4 → FUMING SULPHURIC ACID (OLEUM)

Adding sulphur trioxide directly to water produces sulphuric acid. However the reaction produces an ACID MIST which is difficult to contain and control, and so ...

- The SULPHUR TRIOXIDE is dissolved in CONCENTRATED SULPHURIC ACID to form FUMING SULPHURIC ACID, known as OLEUM.

$$SULPHUR\ TRIOXIDE + CONCENTRATED\ SULPHURIC\ ACID \longrightarrow OLEUM : SO_{3(g)} + H_2SO_{4(l)} \longrightarrow H_2S_2O_{7(l)}$$

4 OLEUM → WATER IS CAREFULLY ADDED → CONCENTRATED SULPHURIC ACID

- WATER is then very carefully added to the OLEUM to produce CONCENTRATED SULPHURIC ACID (about 98%)

$$OLEUM + WATER \longrightarrow CONCENTRATED\ SULPHURIC\ ACID : H_2S_2O_{7(l)} + H_2O_{(l)} \longrightarrow 2H_2SO_{4(l)}$$

Concentrated Sulphuric Acid As A Dehydrating Agent

Dehydration is the removal of water or the elements of water from a compound.
Concentrated sulphuric acid can be used as a dehydrating agent, for example ...

- If conc. H_2SO_4 is added to some organic compounds containing HYDROGEN and OXYGEN it removes the elements of water from the compound leaving CARBON. If we add conc. H_2SO_4 to sugar ...

- If conc. H_2SO_4 is added to HYDRATED COPPER SULPHATE crystals it removes the water of crystallisation to leave behind ANHYDROUS COPPER SULPHATE.

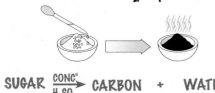

$$SUGAR \xrightarrow[H_2SO_4]{CONC^N} CARBON + WATER$$

$$HYDRATED\ COPPER\ SULPHATE \xrightarrow[H_2SO_4]{CONC^N} ANHYDROUS\ COPPER\ SULPHATE + WATER$$

There are many chemical principles involved in the manufacture of sulphuric acid ...

Oxidation Reactions

The addition of oxygen to a substance is known as OXIDATION. The manufacture of sulphuric acid involves an oxidation reaction ...

... at STEP 1 where SULPHUR is oxidised to produce SULPHUR DIOXIDE and also ...

... at STEP 2 where SULPHUR DIOXIDE is oxidised to produce SULPHUR TRIOXIDE (see below).

Exothermic Reactions

Reactions that transfer HEAT ENERGY to the surroundings are known as EXOTHERMIC reactions. Both of the oxidation reactions above, as well as the reaction between OLEUM and WATER to produce CONCENTRATED SULPHURIC ACID, are exothermic reactions.

Effect Of Energy Transfer, Rates Of Reaction And Equilibrium Conditions On Reversible Reactions

The manufacture of SULPHUR TRIOXIDE in STEP 2 is a REVERSIBLE REACTION involving ...

• ENERGY TRANSFERS associated with the breaking and formation of chemical bonds. Less energy is needed to break the bonds in the sulphur dioxide and oxygen molecules than is released in the formation of the sulphur trioxide molecules.

$$\overset{\text{ENDOTHERMIC}}{\longleftarrow} \quad 2SO_{2(g)} + O_{2(g)} \underset{\text{REVERSE}}{\overset{\text{FORWARD}}{\rightleftharpoons}} 2SO_{3(g)} \quad \overset{\text{EXOTHERMIC}}{\longrightarrow}$$

If we consider the atoms involved ...

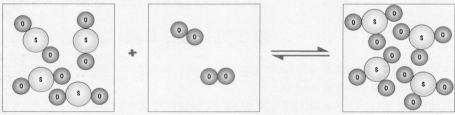

In a closed system the above reaction would reach a state of DYNAMIC EQUILIBRIUM, where the rate of the forward reaction is equal to the rate of the backward reaction. Adding EXCESS AIR will 'push' the reaction from left to right and so increase the yield.

EFFECT OF TEMPERATURE

Because the formation of sulphur trioxide is exothermic, a LOW TEMPERATURE WOULD FAVOUR THE PRODUCTION OF SULPHUR TRIOXIDE ie. it favours the forward reaction which would increase the yield. A high temperature would increase the rate of reaction equally in both directions, in other words it would make the sulphur trioxide form faster and also break down faster. Therefore a compromise of about 450°C is used to ensure a good yield and also a decent rate of reaction. The graph opposite is typical of how temperature affects the % yield of SO_3.

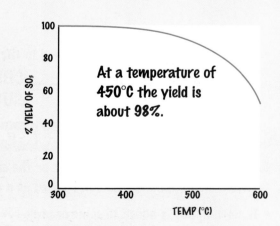

At a temperature of 450°C the yield is about 98%.

EFFECT OF CATALYST

The use of VANADIUM OXIDE, V_2O_5, increases the rate of production of SO_3.

EFFECT OF PRESSURE

Since three molecules are being changed into two molecules, increasing the pressure favours the smaller volume. However a high pressure would cause the sulphur dioxide to liquify and so a relatively low pressure of between one and two atmospheres is used. Cost and safety are also factors that affect the choice of pressure.

The fact that a temperature of about 450°C gives such a high yield anyway means that there is little need to increase the pressure above the normal atmospheric pressure of 1 atmosphere in order to increase the yield.

Aluminium

ALUMINIUM is a reactive metal that is resistant to corrosion due to the formation of a thin 'skin' of ALUMINIUM OXIDE on its surface.

This 'skin' of oxide is produced by the reaction between the aluminium and oxygen from the air and it prevents further corrosion. It's for this reason that greenhouses don't have to be painted.

However, for some uses of aluminium, a thicker layer of this protective oxide is needed than occurs naturally. This can be done artificially in two stages ...

1 The thin natural layer of the oxide is removed by placing the aluminium in SODIUM HYDROXIDE SOLUTION.

2 The ELECTROLYSIS of DILUTE SULPHURIC ACID is used to coat the aluminium with a thicker layer of the oxide. The aluminium to be coated is made the POSITIVE ELECTRODE (anode). During the electrolysis OXYGEN forms at the surface of the aluminium. A reaction takes place between the aluminium and oxygen, forming a thicker oxide layer. This process is called ANODISING.

Electro-plating

Steel (and most other metals) can be ELECTRO-PLATED. The idea behind this is that a less expensive metal can be given a coat of a more expensive metal. Doing this is cheaper than having an object purely made of the more expensive metal and it may also help to prevent corrosion. If we wanted to electro-plate a steel object with a thin coat of silver ...

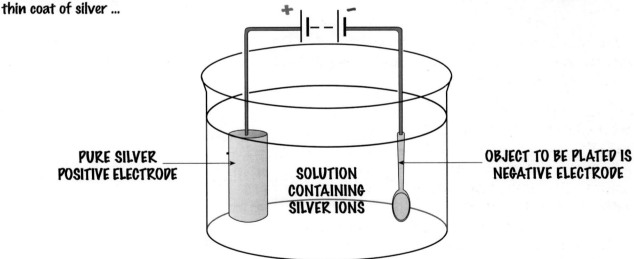

PURE SILVER POSITIVE ELECTRODE

SOLUTION CONTAINING SILVER IONS

OBJECT TO BE PLATED IS NEGATIVE ELECTRODE

- The steel object to be electro-plated forms the NEGATIVE ELECTRODE.
- The POSITIVE ELECTRODE is made of the PURE PLATING METAL, in this case SILVER.
- Both are placed in a SOLUTION containing IONS of the PLATING METAL, in this case it would be a solution of SILVER NITRATE.

When a current passes through the solution SILVER IONS pass into solution ...
... at the POSITIVE ELECTRODE.
SILVER IONS move towards the NEGATIVE ELECTRODE to form SILVER ATOMS ...
... which stick to the steel object, coating it in SILVER.

Other plating metals include NICKEL and GOLD.

IRON is an important metal. However its properties can be changed by adding small quantities of CARBON or OTHER METALS to make STEEL. Steel is an ALLOY since it is a mixture of iron with carbon or other metals.

Molten iron obtained from a blast furnace is impure and contains roughly 5% of CARBON and OTHER METALS. This iron is very brittle with limited uses. In order to reduce the content of these impurities and change the iron into steel it is transferred to another furnace where ...

... it is MIXED with RECYCLED SCRAP IRON and ...

... PURE OXYGEN is passed into the mixture.

The oxygen reacts with non-metal impurities such as carbon, silicon and sulphur which are converted into ACIDIC OXIDES.

CALCIUM CARBONATE (limestone) is then added to remove some of the acidic oxides as slag which is tapped off along with the steel when the furnace is tilted. Other acidic oxides such as carbon dioxide are gases and are collected separately.

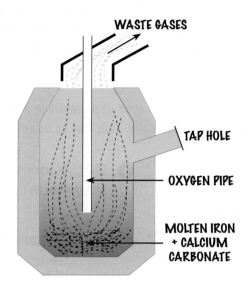

WASTE GASES

TAP HOLE

OXYGEN PIPE

MOLTEN IRON + CALCIUM CARBONATE

Properties Of Steel

The quantity of CARBON and/or OTHER ELEMENTS determine the properties of the steel obtained. Calculated quantities may even be added to make a wide range of steels eg.

Steel with a HIGH CARBON content is strong but brittle.

Steel with a LOW CARBON content is SOFT and EASILY SHAPED. MILD STEEL is easily pressed into shape.

Steel which contains CHROMIUM and NICKEL is called STAINLESS STEEL. It is hard and resistant to corrosion.

Chemical Principles Involved In The Manufacture Of Steel

The manufacture of steel involves some important chemical principles ...

❶ The addition of oxygen to a substance is known as OXIDATION. In the production of steel from impure iron PURE OXYGEN is passed into the mixture which reacts with non-metal impurities to form OXIDES.

$$\text{SILICON} + \text{OXYGEN} \longrightarrow \text{SILICON OXIDE}$$
$$Si_{(s)} + O_{2(g)} \longrightarrow SiO_{2(s)}$$

❷ The silicon oxide, SiO_2, formed by the oxidation of silicon is an ACIDIC OXIDE.
In order to remove this impurity, CALCIUM CARBONATE (limestone) is added to the mixture. The calcium carbonate decomposes to form CALCIUM OXIDE.

$$\text{CALCIUM CARBONATE} \longrightarrow \text{CALCIUM OXIDE} + \text{CARBON DIOXIDE}$$

The calcium oxide formed is a BASIC OXIDE and it reacts with the silicon oxide to form calcium silicate or slag which is tapped off.

$$\text{SILICON OXIDE} + \text{CALCIUM OXIDE} \longrightarrow \text{CALCIUM SILICATE}$$
$$SiO_{2(s)} + CaO_{(s)} \longrightarrow CaSiO_{3(l)}$$
$$\text{(acidic oxide)} \quad \text{(basic oxide)} \quad \text{(slag)}$$

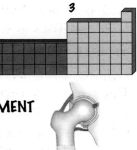

Titanium And Its Uses

TITANIUM is a TRANSITION METAL, one of a block of metallic elements situated between Groups 2 and 3 of the periodic table. It is STRONG and RESISTANT TO CORROSION. It is used ...

... in AEROPLANES    ... in NUCLEAR REACTORS   ... for REPLACEMENT HIP JOINTS

Extraction Of Titanium From Its Ores

The raw material for the extraction of titanium is the ore RUTILE which contains TITANIUM DIOXIDE, TiO_2. There are TWO steps in its extraction ...

1   TITANIUM DIOXIDE → CONVERTED TO ... → TITANIUM CHLORIDE

- TITANIUM DIOXIDE is converted into TITANIUM CHLORIDE, $TiCl_4$ (you don't need to know any details).

2   TITANIUM CHLORIDE → DISPLACED BY SODIUM OR MAGNESIUM → TITANIUM

- The TITANIUM CHLORIDE is then reacted with SODIUM (or MAGNESIUM) ...
  ... to form TITANIUM metal and SODIUM CHLORIDE (or MAGNESIUM CHLORIDE).
- The reaction is carried out in an atmosphere of the noble gas ARGON.

TITANIUM CHLORIDE + SODIUM $\longrightarrow$ TITANIUM + SODIUM CHLORIDE

$$TiCl_{4(l)} + 4Na_{(s)} \longrightarrow Ti_{(s)} + 4NaCl_{(s)}$$

Or ...

TITANIUM CHLORIDE + MAGNESIUM $\longrightarrow$ TITANIUM + MAGNESIUM CHLORIDE

$$TiCl_{4(l)} + 2Mg_{(s)} \longrightarrow Ti_{(s)} + 2MgCl_{2(s)}$$

Chemical Principles Involved In The Extraction Of Titanium

The extraction of titanium involves some important chemical principles ...

1 The REACTIVITY SERIES places metals in order of their reactivity. Titanium is <u>below</u> both sodium and magnesium in the series. Consequently when either sodium or magnesium are reacted with titanium chloride a DISPLACEMENT REACTION takes place where the titanium in titanium chloride is displaced by the sodium or magnesium.

2 The above displacement reaction is carried out in an atmosphere of ARGON. Argon is a noble gas which is UNREACTIVE and provides an INERT atmosphere. This ensures that no other unwanted reactions take place eg. in an atmosphere of air, oxidation would occur.

3 The GAIN OF ELECTRONS by a substance is known as REDUCTION. In the extraction process above we started off with titanium dioxide which contains TITANIUM IONS, Ti^{4+}, and we ended up with titanium atoms, Ti. In other words each titanium ion has gained FOUR ELECTRONS to become a titanium atom.

$$Ti^{4+} + 4e^- \longrightarrow Ti$$

TITANIUM ION   FOUR ELECTRONS   TITANIUM ATOM

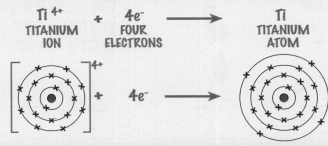

A range of chemical tests can be carried out for the detection and identification of elements and compounds.

Flame Tests

LITHIUM, SODIUM, POTASSIUM, CALCIUM and BARIUM COMPOUNDS can be recognised by their distinctive colours in a flame test. The procedure is as follows ...

A piece of nichrome wire is dipped in concentrated hydrochloric acid to clean it.

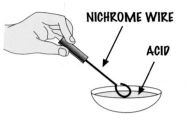

NICHROME WIRE

ACID

It is dipped in the compound and then put into a bunsen flame to give us the following distinctive colours ...

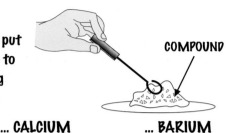

COMPOUND

... LITHIUM (red)   ... SODIUM (yellow)   ... POTASSIUM (lilac)   ... CALCIUM (brick-red)   ... BARIUM (apple-green)

Reaction Of Carbonates With Dilute Acid

CARBONATES react with DILUTE ACIDS ...
... to form CARBON DIOXIDE gas ...
... (and a 'salt' and water).

eg. If we add CALCIUM CARBONATE ...
... to DILUTE HYDROCHLORIC ACID...
... then the carbonate will 'fizz' as it reacts with the acid giving off CARBON DIOXIDE.

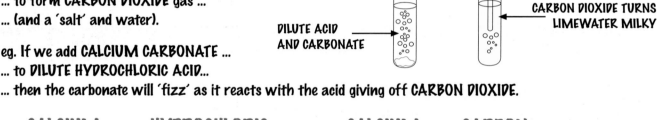

DILUTE ACID AND CARBONATE

CARBON DIOXIDE TURNS LIMEWATER MILKY

CALCIUM CARBONATE + HYDROCHLORIC ACID ⟶ CALCIUM CHLORIDE + CARBON DIOXIDE + WATER

$$CaCO_{3(s)} + 2HCl_{(aq)} \longrightarrow CaCl_{2(aq)} + CO_{2(g)} + H_2O_{(l)}$$

Thermal Decomposition Of Copper And Zinc Carbonate

When COPPER CARBONATE and ZINC CARBONATE are heated a THERMAL DECOMPOSITION reaction takes place resulting in a distinctive colour change which enables identification of the two compounds.

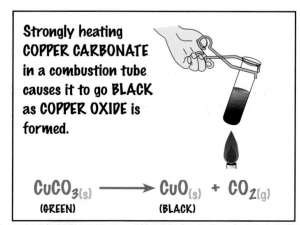

Strongly heating COPPER CARBONATE in a combustion tube causes it to go BLACK as COPPER OXIDE is formed.

$$CuCO_{3(s)} \longrightarrow CuO_{(s)} + CO_{2(g)}$$
(GREEN)   (BLACK)

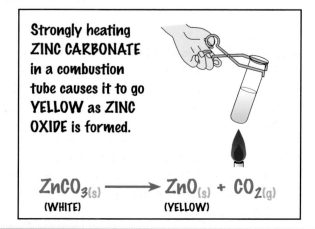

Strongly heating ZINC CARBONATE in a combustion tube causes it to go YELLOW as ZINC OXIDE is formed.

$$ZnCO_{3(s)} \longrightarrow ZnO_{(s)} + CO_{2(g)}$$
(WHITE)   (YELLOW)

Metal Ions

METAL COMPOUNDS in solution contain METAL IONS. Some of these form PRECIPITATES ie. insoluble solids that 'come out' of solution when SODIUM HYDROXIDE SOLUTION is added to them.

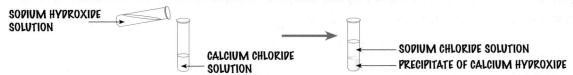

SODIUM HYDROXIDE SOLUTION

CALCIUM CHLORIDE SOLUTION

SODIUM CHLORIDE SOLUTION
PRECIPITATE OF CALCIUM HYDROXIDE

In the example above a white precipitate of CALCIUM HYDROXIDE is formed (and sodium chloride solution). If we consider the IONS involved in the formation of the precipitate ...

$$Ca^{2+}_{(aq)} \quad + \quad 2OH^-_{(aq)} \quad \longrightarrow \quad Ca(OH)_{2(s)}$$

(FROM THE CALCIUM CHLORIDE)   (FROM THE SODIUM HYDROXIDE)   (FORMED AS A PRECIPITATE)

The following ions form white precipitates with sodium hydroxide solution ...

METAL ION	PRECIPITATE FORMED	COLOUR OF PRECIPITATE
ALUMINIUM, $Al^{3+}_{(aq)}$	ALUMINIUM HYDROXIDE: $Al^{3+}_{(aq)} + 3OH^-_{(aq)} \longrightarrow Al(OH)_{3(s)}$	WHITE
CALCIUM, $Ca^{2+}_{(aq)}$	CALCIUM HYDROXIDE: $Ca^{2+}_{(aq)} + 2OH^-_{(aq)} \longrightarrow Ca(OH)_{2(s)}$	WHITE
MAGNESIUM, $Mg^{2+}_{(aq)}$	MAGNESIUM HYDROXIDE: $Mg^{2+}_{(aq)} + 2OH^-_{(aq)} \longrightarrow Mg(OH)_{2(s)}$	WHITE

... but only the ALUMINIUM HYDROXIDE precipitate dissolves in excess sodium hydroxide solution, ...
... while the following ions form coloured precipitates with sodium hydroxide solution.

COPPER$_{(II)}$ $Cu^{2+}_{(aq)}$	COPPER$_{(II)}$ HYDROXIDE: $Cu^{2+}_{(aq)} + 2OH^-_{(aq)} \longrightarrow Cu(OH)_{2(s)}$	BLUE
IRON$_{(II)}$ $Fe^{2+}_{(aq)}$	IRON$_{(II)}$ HYDROXIDE: $Fe^{2+}_{(aq)} + 2OH^-_{(aq)} \longrightarrow Fe(OH)_{2(s)}$	GREEN
IRON$_{(III)}$ $Fe^{3+}_{(aq)}$	IRON$_{(III)}$ HYDROXIDE: $Fe^{3+}_{(aq)} + 3OH^-_{(aq)} \longrightarrow Fe(OH)_{3(s)}$	BROWN

Chloride And Sulphate Ions

The tests for these two ions both produce a WHITE PRECIPITATE.

- CHLORIDE IONS in solution form a WHITE PRECIPITATE of SILVER CHLORIDE if a few drops of DILUTE NITRIC ACID are added, followed by a few drops of SILVER NITRATE SOLUTION.

$$Ag^+_{(aq)} + Cl^-_{(aq)} \longrightarrow AgCl_{(s)}$$

- SULPHATE IONS in solution form a WHITE PRECIPITATE of BARIUM CHLORIDE if a few drops of DILUTE HYDROCHLORIC ACID are added, followed by a few drops of BARIUM CHLORIDE SOLUTION.

$$Ba^{2+}_{(aq)} + SO_4^{2-}_{(aq)} \longrightarrow BaSO_{4(s)}$$

Ammonium, Nitrate, Bromide And Iodide Ions

If SODIUM HYDROXIDE is added to AMMONIUM IONS, NH_4^+, in solution, AMMONIA gas is given off.
A test for ammonia gas is that it TURNS DAMP LITMUS PAPER BLUE.

NITRATE IONS in solution are REDUCED to AMMONIUM IONS if SODIUM HYDROXIDE SOLUTION is added followed by ALUMINIUM POWDER.

BROMIDE and IODIDE IONS in solution form COLOURED PRECIPITATES if a few drops of DILUTE NITRIC ACID are added followed by a few drops of SILVER NITRATE SOLUTION.

$$Ag^+_{(aq)} + Br^-_{(aq)} \longrightarrow AgBr_{(s)}$$
(pale yellow)

$$Ag^+_{(aq)} + I^-_{(aq)} \longrightarrow AgI_{(s)}$$
(yellow)

Why Use Instrumental Techniques?

Before the development of instrumental methods of analysis, standard laboratory equipment was used in ways similar to the ones we use in school. Instruments have the following advantages ...

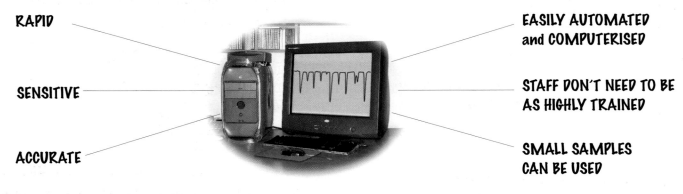

RAPID

SENSITIVE

ACCURATE

EASILY AUTOMATED and COMPUTERISED

STAFF DON'T NEED TO BE AS HIGHLY TRAINED

SMALL SAMPLES CAN BE USED

Mass Spectrometry – Identifies Elements

It can also be used for compounds but as far as your examination is concerned you should give MASS SPECTROMETRY as an instrumental method of identifying ELEMENTS. It relies on measuring the deflection of ions of the substance as they pass through the magnetic field of the spectrometer.

Infra-red Spectroscopy – Identifies Compounds

It does this by identifying the functional groups present in the molecule based on the frequency of vibration of the bonds present. Luckily all you need to know is the name of this technique.

Drawbacks Of The Above Techniques

- Integrity of the sample: The sample must be completely pure as even the tiniest traces of other substances would be detected.
- Calibration of the machine: All the settings of the machine must be checked meticulously before use, using standard samples of known purity.

Industrial Applications

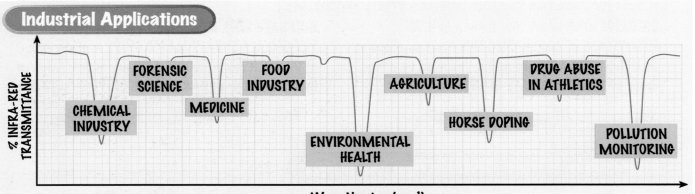

% INFRA-RED TRANSMITTANCE

FORENSIC SCIENCE

FOOD INDUSTRY

DRUG ABUSE IN ATHLETICS

CHEMICAL INDUSTRY

MEDICINE

AGRICULTURE

HORSE DOPING

ENVIRONMENTAL HEALTH

POLLUTION MONITORING

Wave Number (cm⁻¹)

Rapid progress in electronics and computing have provided the basis for the development of accurate instrumental methods of analysing substances. In addition there is now greater interest in the quick and effective monitoring of changes in environmental conditions. At its simplest this can be seen easily enough in emission detecting equipment in garages. Developments in fibre optics and magnetometry have also made equipment more sophisticated.

ADVANCES IN TECHNOLOGY ... ... have led to ...

- INCREASED MINIATURISATION
- GREATER SENSITIVITY
- EASE OF USE
- GREATER AUTOMATION
- GREATER VERSATILITY

SULPHURIC ACID

SULPHURIC ACID is used ...

... as the acid in **CAR BATTERIES** ... to make **DETERGENTS** ... to make **FERTILISERS**

MANUFACTURE OF SULPHURIC ACID

The three raw materials are **SULPHUR, AIR AND WATER**.

① SULPHUR — BURNT IN AIR → SULPHUR DIOXIDE

SULPHUR + OXYGEN $\longrightarrow$ SULPHUR DIOXIDE : $S_{(s)} + O_{2(g)} \longrightarrow SO_{2(g)}$

② SULPHUR DIOXIDE — MORE AIR AND V_2O_5 → SULPHUR TRIOXIDE

SULPHUR DIOXIDE + OXYGEN $\rightleftharpoons$ SULPHUR TRIOXIDE : $2SO_{2(g)} + O_{2(g)} \rightleftharpoons 2SO_{3(g)}$

A catalyst of **VANADIUM OXIDE**, a temp. of about 450°C and a pressure of 1 to 2 ATMOSPHERES are used.

③ SULPHUR TRIOXIDE — DISSOLVED IN CONC^N. H_2SO_4 → FUMING SULPHURIC ACID (OLEUM)

SULPHUR TRIOXIDE + CONCENTRATED SULPHURIC ACID $\longrightarrow$ OLEUM : $SO_{3(g)} + H_2SO_{4(l)} \longrightarrow H_2S_2O_{7(l)}$

④ OLEUM — WATER IS CAREFULLY ADDED → CONCENTRATED SULPHURIC ACID

OLEUM + WATER $\longrightarrow$ CONCENTRATED SULPHURIC ACID: $H_2S_2O_{7(l)} + H_2O_{(l)} \longrightarrow 2H_2SO_{4(l)}$

CONC^N SULPHURIC ACID AS A DEHYDRATING AGENT

Concentrated H_2SO_4 can be used to remove water from a compound.

SUGAR $\xrightarrow[H_2SO_4]{CONC^N}$ CARBON + WATER

HYDRATED COPPER SULPHATE $\xrightarrow[H_2SO_4]{CONC^N}$ ANHYDROUS COPPER SULPHATE + WATER

CHEMICAL PRINCIPLES INVOLVED IN MANUFACTURE OF H_2SO_4

OXIDATION REACTIONS
• Sulphur is oxidised to produce **SULPHUR DIOXIDE**.
• Sulphur dioxide is oxidised to produce **SULPHUR TRIOXIDE**.

EXOTHERMIC REACTIONS
Both of the above are exothermic reactions. The reaction between **OLEUM** and **WATER** to produce **CONC^N** H_2SO_4 is also exothermic.

THE MANUFACTURE OF SULPHUR TRIOXIDE

$\longleftarrow$ ENDOTHERMIC $\quad 2SO_{2(g)} + O_{2(g)} \xrightarrow[\text{REVERSE}]{\text{FORWARD}} 2SO_{3(g)} \quad$ EXOTHERMIC $\longrightarrow$

ENERGY TRANSFERS INVOLVED ... less energy is needed to break the bonds in the sulphur dioxide and oxygen molecules than is released in the formation of the sulphur trioxide molecules.

EFFECT OF TEMPERATURE ... because the formation of SO_3 is exothermic, **LOW TEMP WOULD FAVOUR ITS PRODUCTION**, ie. favours the forward reaction which would increase the yield. A **HIGH TEMP** increases the rate of reaction equally in both directions. A compromise of about 450°C is used.

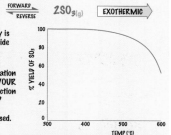

EFFECT OF CATALYST ... vanadium oxide, V_2O_5, is used to increase the rate of production of SO_3.

EFFECT OF PRESSURE ... since three molecules are being changed to two, increasing the pressure favours the smaller volume.
However a high pressure causes the SO_3 to liquify. A pressure just above the normal atmospheric pressure of 1 atmosphere is used.

ALUMINIUM AND TITANIUM

ALUMINIUM

A reactive metal that is resistant to corrosion due to the formation of a 'thin' skin of **ALUMINIUM OXIDE** on its surface. A thicker layer of this oxide can be artificially added to the aluminium in 2 stages.

① The thin layer of oxide is removed by placing the aluminium in **SODIUM HYDROXIDE SOLUTION**.

② The **ELECTROLYSIS of DILUTE SULPHURIC ACID** is used to coat the aluminium with a thicker layer of the oxide.

TITANIUM

A **TRANSITION METAL, STRONG** and **RESISTANT TO CORROSION**. It is used ...

... in **AEROPLANES** ... in **NUCLEAR REACTORS** ... for **REPLACEMENT HIP JOINTS**

EXTRACTION OF TITANIUM

The raw material is the ore **RUTILE**. It contains **TITANIUM DIOXIDE** which is firstly converted to **TITANIUM CHLORIDE**. Titanium chloride is then reacted with **SODIUM (or MAGNESIUM)** to form **TITANIUM** metal and NaCl or $MgCl_2$.

TITANIUM CHLORIDE + **SODIUM** $\longrightarrow$ **TITANIUM** + **SODIUM CHLORIDE**

• Titanium is below both sodium and magnesium in the reactivity series and so a displacement reaction takes place.
• Reaction is carried out in the unreactive and inert atmosphere of **ARGON**.
• Titanium dioxide is **REDUCED** to become titanium metal where each titanium ion gains 4 electrons to become a titanium atom.

IRON, STEEL AND ELECTRO-PLATING

IRON AND STEEL
Molten iron obtained from a blast furnace is impure and contains roughly 5% **CARBON** and **OTHER METALS**.
To change **IRON** into **STEEL** ...
... it is mixed with **RECYCLED SCRAP METAL** and ...
... **PURE OXYGEN** is passed into the mixture.
CALCIUM CARBONATE is added to remove some of the acidic oxides as slag.

WASTE GASES / TAP HOLE / OXYGEN PIPE / MOLTEN IRON + CALCIUM CARBONATE

PROPERTIES OF STEEL

Steel with a **HIGH CARBON** content is strong but brittle.

Steel with a **LOW CARBON** content is **SOFT and EASILY SHAPED. MILD STEEL** is easily pressed into shape.

Steel which contains **CHROMIUM** and **NICKEL** is called **STAINLESS STEEL**. It is hard and resistant to corrosion.

CHEMICAL PRINCIPLES INVOLVED IN THE MANUFACTURE

① **OXIDATION** reactions, eg ...

SILICON + OXYGEN $\longrightarrow$ SILICON OXIDE

② **ACID-BASE** reactions ...

SILICON OXIDE + CALCIUM OXIDE $\longrightarrow$ CALCIUM SILICATE
(acidic oxide)   (basic oxide)   (slag)

ELECTRO-PLATING

A less expensive metal can be coated with a more expensive metal. The object to be plated forms the **NEGATIVE ELECTRODE**. The **POSITIVE ELECTRODE** is made of the **PURE PLATING METAL** and both are placed in a solution containing **IONS of the PLATING METAL**.

PURE SILVER POSITIVE ELECTRODE / SOLUTION CONTAINING SILVER IONS / OBJECT TO BE PLATED IS NEGATIVE ELECTRODE

DETECTION AND IDENTIFICATION OF ELEMENTS AND COMPOUNDS

FLAME TESTS
LITHIUM (red), **SODIUM** (yellow), **POTASSIUM** (lilac), **CALCIUM** (brick-red) and **BARIUM** (apple-green) COMPOUNDS can be recognised by their distinctive colours in a flame test.

REACTION OF CARBONATES WITH DILUTE ACID
CARBONATES react with **DILUTE ACIDS** to form **CARBON DIOXIDE** (and a 'salt' and water).

CALCIUM CARBONATE + HYDROCHLORIC ACID $\longrightarrow$ CALCIUM CHLORIDE + CARBON DIOXIDE + WATER

$CaCO_{3(s)} + 2HCl_{(aq)} \longrightarrow CaCl_{2(aq)} + CO_{2(g)} + H_2O_{(l)}$

THERMAL DECOMPOSITION OF COPPER AND ZINC CARBONATE

$CuCO_{3(s)} \longrightarrow CuO_{(s)} + CO_{2(g)}$ $ZnCO_{3(s)} \longrightarrow ZnO_{(s)} + CO_{2(g)}$
(GREEN) (BLACK)   (WHITE) (YELLOW)

METAL IONS
Metal compounds in solution contain metal ions. Some of these form **PRECIPITATES** when **SODIUM HYDROXIDE SOLUTION** is added to them.

METAL ION	$Al^{3+}_{(aq)}$	$Ca^{2+}_{(aq)}$	$Mg^{2+}_{(aq)}$	$Cu^{2+}_{(aq)}$	$Fe^{2+}_{(aq)}$	$Fe^{3+}_{(aq)}$
COLOUR OF PRECIPITATE	WHITE	WHITE	WHITE	BLUE	GREEN	BROWN

CHLORIDE AND SULPHATE IONS
Both of these form white precipitates ...

$Ag^+_{(aq)} + Cl^-_{(aq)} \longrightarrow AgCl_{(s)}$ $Ba^{2+}_{(aq)} + SO_4^{2-}_{(aq)} \longrightarrow BaSO_{4(s)}$

AMMONIUM, NITRATE, BROMIDE AND IODIDE IONS
• Sodium hydroxide is added to $NH^{4+}_{(aq)}$ ions, ammonia is given off.
• Nitrate ions in sol^n are reduced to $NH_{4(aq)}^+$ ions if $NaOH_{(aq)}$ is added followed by aluminium powder.
• $Br^-_{(aq)}$ and $I^-_{(aq)}$ ions form coloured precipitates if a few drops of dilute nitric acid are added followed by a few drops of silver nitrate sol^n.

INSTRUMENTAL METHODS OF DETECTION

WHY WE USE INSTRUMENTAL TECHNIQUES
Before the development of instrumental methods of analysis, standard laboratory equipment was used in ways similar to the ones we use in school. Instruments have the following advantages ...
• **RAPID**   • **EASILY AUTOMATED and COMPUTERISED**   • **SENSITIVE**
• **ACCURATE**   • **STAFF DON'T NEED TO BE AS HIGHLY TRAINED**   • **SMALL SAMPLES CAN BE USED**

IDENTIFYING ELEMENTS AND COMPOUNDS
• **MASS SPECTROMETRY** can be used for identifying **ELEMENTS** (it can also be used to identify compounds).
• **INFRA-RED SPECTROSCOPY** can be used for identifying **COMPOUNDS**.

DRAWBACKS OF THE ABOVE TECHNIQUES
• **Integrity of the sample:** The sample must be completely pure as even the tiniest traces of other substances would be detected.
• **Calibration of the machine:** All the settings of the machine must be checked meticulously before use, using standard samples of known purity.

INDUSTRIAL APPLICATIONS

CHEMICAL INDUSTRY / FORENSIC SCIENCE / MEDICINE / FOOD INDUSTRY / ENVIRONMENTAL HEALTH / AGRICULTURE / HORSE DOPING / DRUG ABUSE IN ATHLETICS / POLLUTION MONITORING

• Rapid progress in electronics and computing have provided the basis for the development of accurate instrumental methods of analysing substances. Developments in fibre optics and magnetometry have also made equipment more sophisticated.

ADVANCES IN TECHNOLOGY ... have led to ...
• **INCREASED MINIATURISATION**   • **GREATER AUTOMATION**
• **GREATER SENSITIVITY**   • **GREATER VERSATILITY**
• **EASE OF USE**

1. 'The industrial development of a country can be measured by the amount of sulphuric acid they use every year.' Explain the significance of the statement.

2. a) What are the three raw materials used in the manufacture of sulphuric acid.
b) Complete the following word and symbol equations (including state symbols) for the four steps in the manufacture of sulphuric acid.
   i) SULPHUR + OXYGEN ⟶
   : _____ + $O_{2(g)}$ ⟶
   ii) SULPHUR DIOXIDE + OXYGEN ⇌ (CONC^n)
   : _____ + $O_{2(g)}$ ⇌
   iii) SULPHUR TRIOXIDE + SULPHURIC ACID ⟶
   : _____ + $H_2SO_{4(l)}$ ⟶
   iv) OLEUM + WATER ⟶
   : _____ + $H_2O_{(l)}$ ⟶
c) i) At what temperature and pressure does the reaction at step b) ii) take place?
   ii) What is the purpose of using a catalyst of vanadium oxide at this stage?
d) At step b) iii) sulphur trioxide could be added directly to water to produce sulphuric acid. Why is this reaction not carried out?

3. a) Concentrated sulphuric acid can be used as a dehydrating agent. Explain what this means.
b) The diagram opposite shows concentrated sulphuric acid being added to sugar. Explain, with the aid of a word equation, what would be observed.

4. a) Which reactions in the manufacture of sulphuric acid are oxidation reactions? Explain your choice.
b) Which reactions in the manufacture of sulphuric acid are exothermic reactions? Explain your choice.
c) i) The table below gives the % yield of sulphur trioxide and temperature of reaction.

TEMPERATURE (°C)	300	350	400	450	500	550	600
% YIELD OF SO_3	100	100	100	98	94	82	50

Draw a graph to show the data.
   ii) Explain why sulphur trioxide is produced at a temperature of 450°C.
   iii) What happens to the % yield of SO_3 if the temperature is increased above 450°C?
d) The % yield of SO_3 can be increased by increasing the pressure. However a low pressure of between one and two atmospheres is used. Explain why.

5. a) Why is aluminium resistant to corrosion?
b) Explain the process of anodising.

6. a) What are the advantages of electro-plating a metal such as steel?
b) The diagram opposite shows an arrangement that can be used to electro-plate a steel object with a thin coat of silver.
   i) Why is the positive electrode made of pure silver?
   ii) Why is the object to be plated made the negative electrode?
   iii) Why are the two electrodes placed in a solution containing silver ions?

PURE SILVER POSITIVE ELECTRODE
OBJECT TO BE PLATED IS NEGATIVE ELECTRODE
SOLUTION CONTAINING SILVER IONS

7. a) Steel is an alloy of iron. Explain what this means.
b) Why does the iron obtained from a blast furnace have limited uses?
c) Steel is made by mixing iron from a blast furnace with recycled scrap iron. Pure oxygen is then passed into the mixture. Explain why.
d) What is the purpose of then adding calcium carbonate?

WASTE GASES

8. a) What properties does steel with a high carbon content have?
b) What properties does steel with a low carbon content have?
c) What properties does steel which contains chromium and nickel have?

9. a) Complete the following word equations showing two reactions which occur inside the furnace.
   i) SILICON + OXYGEN ⟶
   ii) SILICON OXIDE + CALCIUM OXIDE ⟶
b) For each reaction above write a balanced symbol equation including state symbols.

10. a) Give two properties of titanium.
b) Give three uses for titanium.

11. a) What is the name of the ore from which titanium is extracted?
b) Complete the following word and symbol equations which show two possible reactions for the production of titanium from titanium chloride.
   i) TITANIUM CHLORIDE + SODIUM ⟶
   ii) TITANIUM CHLORIDE + MAGNESIUM ⟶

12. a) Why is it important that both sodium and magnesium are above titanium in the reactivity series?
b) Why are the reactions in question 11b) carried out in an atmosphere of argon?
c) Why is the extraction of titanium from its ores a reduction reaction? Explain your answer by drawing electron configurations for the relevant particles.

13. a) Name three compounds that can be recognised by their distinctive colours in a flame test.
b) In the procedure for this test a piece of nichrome wire is firstly dipped in concentrated acid. Explain why.
c) For the three compounds you have chosen in part a) what distinctive colours would you get if you carried out the flame test using these compounds.

14. Test tube 'A' in the diagram opposite contains calcium carbonate and hydrochloric acid. Test tube 'B' contains limewater.
a) Write down a word and balanced symbol equation (including state symbols) for the reaction taking place in test tube 'A'.
b) What would you observe happening in test tube 'B'? Explain your answer.

'A'   'B'

15. a) What is a thermal decomposition reaction?
b) i) Explain what you would observe if copper carbonate is strongly heated in a combustion tube.
   ii) Write a balanced symbol equation (including state symbols) for the reaction taking place in a combustion tube.
c) i) Explain what you would observe if zinc carbonate is strongly heated in a combustion tube.
   ii) Write a balanced symbol equation (including state symbols) for the reaction taking place in a combustion tube.

16. a) Explain what would happen if sodium hydroxide solution is added to a solution containing ...
   i) ALUMINIUM IONS.
   ii) COPPER(II) IONS.
   iii) IRON(III) IONS.
b) For each of the above write an ionic equation for the reaction taking place.
c) In which of the reactions above would the precipitate formed dissolve in excess sodium hydroxide solution.

17. a) Describe a test for a solution which contains chloride ions.
b) Describe a test for a solution which contains sulphate ions.

18. a) i) What would happen if sodium hydroxide is added to a solution containing ammonium ions?
   ii) Describe a simple test for the gas given off in part i).
b) Describe a simple test for the identification of i) nitrate ii) bromide iii) iodide ions.

19. a) i) Name two different instrumental methods that can be used for the identification of elements and for the identification of compounds.
   ii) For each method chosen give one advantage and one disadvantage of choosing this method.

20. a) Give four examples of industrial applications where instrumental methods are used.
b) The development of instrumental methods has been aided by advances in technology. Explain how.

Moments

Forces can be used to turn objects about a pivot. If you were to unscrew a wheel nut using a spanner ...

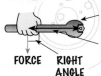

PIVOT

PERPENDICULAR DISTANCE BETWEEN THE LINE OF ACTION OF THE FORCE AND PIVOT.
(This is the shortest distance between the line of action of the force and pivot)

FORCE   RIGHT ANGLE

... the spanner exerts a **MOMENT** or **TURNING FORCE** on the nut given by the formula:

MOMENT (Nm) = FORCE (N) x PERPENDICULAR DISTANCE BETWEEN LINE OF ACTION AND PIVOT (m)

$$\frac{M}{F \times d}$$

There are two ways of increasing the moment or turning force ...

❶ INCREASE THE FORCE APPLIED

❷ INCREASE THE PERPENDICULAR DISTANCE BETWEEN THE LINE OF ACTION OF THE FORCE AND THE PIVOT.

EXAMPLE

The person above exerts a force of 120N and the perpendicular distance from his hand to the pivot is 15cm. What moment does he exert?

Using the formula: MOMENT = FORCE x PERPENDICULAR DISTANCE BETWEEN LINE OF ACTION AND PIVOT
= 120N x 0.15m
= 18Nm

Centre Of Mass

THE CENTRE OF MASS (C of M) of an object is the POINT through which the WHOLE WEIGHT, W, OF THE OBJECT ACTS. If you balance an object on the end of your finger, the point of balance is the centre of mass of the object. For a symmetrical object the centre of mass is to be found along an axis of symmetry.

AXIS OF SYMMETRY   W   CENTRE OF MASS   W

Finding The Centre Of Mass

When an object is suspended it will always come to rest with its centre of mass situated somewhere directly below the point of suspension. In this position the weight of the object does not exert any turning force on the object since the perpendicular distance from the line of action of the force (weight of object) to the pivot (point of suspension) is zero. If we were to repeat with a different point of suspension then we could locate the exact position of the centre of mass. To find the centre of mass of an object such as a thin sheet of material all you would need is a plumbline ...

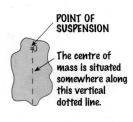

POINT OF SUSPENSION

The centre of mass is situated somewhere along this vertical dotted line.

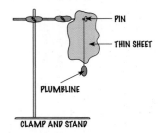

PIN

THIN SHEET

PLUMBLINE

CLAMP AND STAND

PLUMBLINE

CLAMP AND STAND

CENTRE OF MASS

W

- **Hang the SHEET and PLUMBLINE ...**
  ... from one point with ...
  ... both of them free to rotate.
- **Mark position of plumbline ...**
  ... and draw in vertical line.
- **The centre of mass is ...**
  ... somewhere along this line.

- **Repeat with the sheet ...**
  ... and plumbline ...
  ... at a different position.
- **The centre of mass is**
  somewhere along this line.
- **It is at the point where the**
  two lines cross.

- **To check the position ...**
  ... of the centre of mass, ...
  ... try balancing the sheet ...
  ... on the end of your finger ...
  ... at the point where ...
  ... the lines cross.

Law Of Moments

When an object is not turning or is balanced ...

TOTAL CLOCKWISE MOMENTS = TOTAL ANTICLOCKWISE MOMENTS

In other words the total moments of the forces tending to turn the object in a clockwise direction are exactly balanced by the total moments of the forces tending to turn the object in an anticlockwise direction.

The object below is pivoted at its centre of mass. It is supporting two forces, F_1 and F_2.

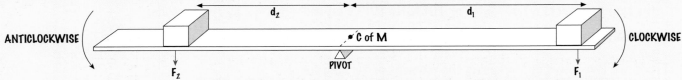

Since the object is balanced ... **TOTAL CLOCKWISE MOMENTS = TOTAL ANTICLOCKWISE MOMENTS**

EXAMPLE 1

ie. $F_1 \times d_1 = F_2 \times d_2$

The diagram below shows the forces acting on a balanced object. It is pivoted at its centre of mass.
Calculate F_2.

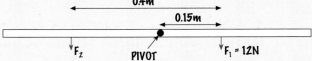

Since the object is balanced ... **TOTAL CLOCKWISE MOMENTS = TOTAL ANTICLOCKWISE MOMENTS**

$$12N \times 0.15m = F_2 \times (0.4 - 0.15)m$$

$$\therefore F_2 = \frac{12N \times 0.15m}{0.25m} = 7.2N$$

EXAMPLE 2

The diagram below shows the forces acting on a balanced object. Calculate the weight of the object.

An important point here is that the object is NOT pivoted at its centre of mass and so the weight of the object exerts a turning force in an anticlockwise direction.

Since the object is balanced ... **TOTAL CLOCKWISE MOMENTS = TOTAL ANTICLOCKWISE MOMENTS**

$$36N \times (0.3 + 0.4)m = W \times 0.4m$$

$$\therefore W = \frac{36N \times 0.7m}{0.4} = 63N$$

Stability

Any object will topple over if the line of action of its weight lies outside its base. When this happens the weight of the object causes a turning effect and the object will tend to fall over. If the line of action of the weight of this car ...

... lies inside its base, there is no problem.

... lies above one edge of the base, the car is on the point of toppling.

... lies outside its base, the car topples over.

The stability of the car above can be increased by having a car with ...

... A LOWER CENTRE OF MASS

... A WIDER WHEEL BASE

This is why racing cars have a low centre of mass <u>and</u> a wide wheel base.

The moon and artificial satellites in orbit around the Earth, the Earth and other planets in orbit around the Sun, electrons in orbit around a nucleus and a rubber ball attached to a piece of string being whirled in a horizontal circle are all examples of objects that travel in circular (or near circular) paths.

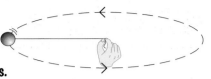

Centripetal Force

If we take a top view of the ball above, which is being whirled in a horizontal circle at a steady speed, you will notice that the direction of motion of the ball constantly changes. The VELOCITY of an object is its speed in a given direction and since the direction of motion of the ball is constantly changing then its velocity is also constantly changing. A force, called the CENTRIPETAL FORCE, which acts towards the centre of the circle, is needed to produce this constant change in velocity. In our example the centripetal force that keeps the ball moving in its circular path is provided by the tension force in the string.

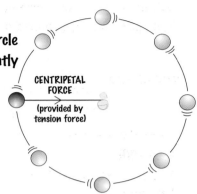

CENTRIPETAL FORCE
(provided by tension force)

The centripetal force needed to keep an object moving in a circular path can vary in the following ways ...

1 THE GREATER THE MASS OF THE OBJECT ...

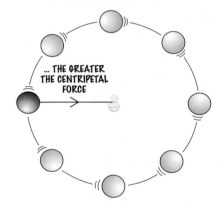

... THE GREATER THE CENTRIPETAL FORCE

2 THE GREATER THE SPEED OF THE OBJECT ...

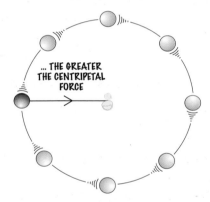

... THE GREATER THE CENTRIPETAL FORCE

3 THE SMALLER THE RADIUS OF THE CIRCLE ...

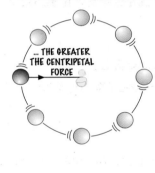

... THE GREATER THE CENTRIPETAL FORCE

Forces At A Distance

Unlike the ball above, not all objects are kept in their orbit by a piece of string, for example ...

... the MOON and ARTIFICIAL SATELLITES are kept in their orbit by the GRAVITATIONAL FORCE OF THE EARTH.

ARTIFICIAL SATELLITE — EARTH

MOON

... the EARTH and OTHER PLANETS are kept in their orbit by the GRAVITATIONAL FORCE OF THE SUN.

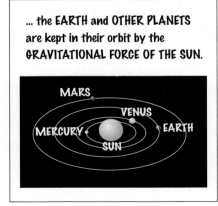

MARS
VENUS
MERCURY
EARTH
SUN

... ELECTRONS are kept in their orbit by the ELECTROSTATIC FORCE OF THE NUCLEUS.

ELECTRONS

NUCLEUS

As we have seen, the centripetal force needed to keep an object moving in a circular path depends on many factors. For instance, for an artificial satellite to stay in orbit at a particular distance, it must orbit at a particular speed to balance the gravitational force of the Earth. For satellites at large distances this means orbiting slowly and therefore taking a much longer time to complete an orbit (due to slow speed and huge circumference of orbit!).

What Is Momentum ?

From your previous studies you are already aware that a moving object has kinetic energy. It also has MOMENTUM.

The momentum (like kinetic energy) of an object depends on two things ...
• The MASS OF THE OBJECT (kg)   • The VELOCITY OF THE OBJECT (m/s)
A moving car has momentum as it has both MASS and VELOCITY.

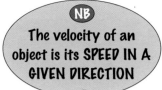

NB
The velocity of an object is its SPEED IN A GIVEN DIRECTION

• If the car now moves ...
... with a GREATER VELOCITY ...
... it has MORE MOMENTUM ...
... providing its mass has not changed.

• However if we have a moving truck ...
... with a GREATER MASS ...
... it may have MORE MOMENTUM ...
... even if its velocity is less than that of the car.

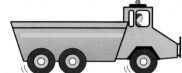

Momentum is a quantity that has both MAGNITUDE (SIZE) and DIRECTION.

Momentum - The Formula

The momentum of an object is calculated using the following formula:

MOMENTUM (kg m/s) = MASS (kg) x VELOCITY (m/s)

... where p is momentum

EXAMPLE 1

The car above has a mass of 1,200kg. It is travelling at a velocity of 30m/s. Calculate its momentum.
Using the formula: MOMENTUM = MASS x VELOCITY
                                    = 1,200kg x 30m/s = 36,000kg m/s

EXAMPLE 2

The truck above has a mass of 4,000kg. Calculate its velocity if it has the same momentum as the car in example 1.

Using the formula: VELOCITY = $\dfrac{\text{MOMENTUM}}{\text{MASS}}$ = $\dfrac{36{,}000\text{kg m/s}}{4000\text{kg}}$ = 9m/s
(rearranged using the formula triangle).

NB Since the truck has a GREATER MASS than the car then ...
... it can move at a SLOWER SPEED and still have the SAME MOMENTUM.

Velocity And Momentum

Velocity and momentum (which is mass x velocity) are both quantities which have MAGNITUDE (size) and DIRECTION. The direction of movement of an object is especially important when it comes to solving numerical problems. To put it simply ...

If car A, below, which is moving from left to right has a POSITIVE VELOCITY and consequently a POSITIVE MOMENTUM, then car B will have a NEGATIVE VELOCITY and NEGATIVE MOMENTUM because it is moving in the opposite direction to car A ie. from right to left.

A    +ve velocity
                         +ve momentum

   -ve velocity    B
   -ve momentum

eg. If A has a mass of 1,000kg
     and a velocity of 20m/s, then ...
     ... its momentum = 1,000kg x 20m/s
                      = 20,000kg m/s

eg. If B has a mass of 1,000kg
     and a velocity of -20m/s, then ...
     ... its momentum = 1,000kg x -20m/s
                      = -20,000kg m/s

Force And Change in Momentum

When two objects collide each exerts a force on the other one. These forces are equal in size and opposite in direction and they result in each object suffering a change of momentum which is also equal in size, but opposite in direction.

The same occurs when a force acts on a moving object; the object will experience a change of momentum for as long as the force is acting.

The extent of the change in momentum depends on the SIZE OF THE FORCE ACTING and the TIME TAKEN FOR THE CHANGE TO OCCUR ie. how long the force is acting.

Force, change in momentum and the time taken for the change are related by the following formula:

$$\text{FORCE (N)} = \frac{\text{CHANGE IN MOMENTUM (kg m/s)}}{\text{TIME (s)}}$$

$$\frac{\Delta(mv)}{F \times t}$$

... where $\Delta(mv)$ is change in momentum.

EXAMPLE

A girl kicks a stationary ball with a force of 30N which acts on the ball for a time of 0.15s.
If the mass of the ball is 0.5kg, calculate
a) the change in momentum of the ball.
b) the increase in velocity of the ball.

a) Using the formula above: CHANGE IN MOMENTUM = FORCE x TIME
(which is rearranged.)

= 30N x 0.15s

= 4.5kg m/s

b)   Change in momentum of the ball = final momentum of the ball - initial momentum of the ball

Initial momentum of the ball = 0, since it is stationary ...

... and so, final momentum of the ball = change in momentum of the ball

= 4.5kg m/s

We can now work out the increase in velocity of the ball using the formula from the previous page.

$$\text{VELOCITY} = \frac{\text{MOMENTUM}}{\text{MASS}} = \frac{4.5\text{kg m/s}}{0.5\text{kg}}$$

= 9m/s (which is the increase in velocity of the ball)

One way that the girl above can increase the change in momentum of the ball and as a result its velocity, without increasing the force applied, is to 'follow through' with her kick. Doing this will increase the time for which the force is applied.

Here are some typical sports where 'follow through' improves velocity ...

... Cricket   ... Golf   ... Football

Collisions And Explosions

In any collision (or explosion), the momentum after the event in a particular direction is the same as the momentum in that direction before the event, PROVIDED THAT NO EXTERNAL FORCES ACT. We say that MOMENTUM IS CONSERVED.

EXAMPLE 1

Two cars are travelling in the same direction along a road. Car A collides with the back of car B and they stick together. Calculate their velocity after the collision.

BEFORE   **AFTER**

A 20m/s   B 9m/s   'v'm/s

1,200 Kg   1,000 Kg   2,200 Kg

$$\text{Momentum before collision} = \text{Momentum of A} + \text{Momentum of B}$$
$$= 1,200\text{kg} \times 20\text{m/s} + 1,000\text{kg} \times 9\text{m/s}$$
$$= 24,000\text{kg m/s} + 9,000\text{kg m/s} = 33,000\text{kg m/s}$$

$$\text{Momentum after collision} = \text{Momentum of A} + \text{B stuck together}$$
$$= 2,200\text{kg} \times \text{'v'm/s} = 2,200v$$

Since momentum is conserved ...

$$\text{TOTAL MOMENTUM BEFORE} = \text{TOTAL MOMENTUM AFTER}$$
$$33,000 = 2,200v$$
$$\therefore v = \frac{33,000}{2,200} = 15\text{m/s}$$

EXAMPLE 2

A gun is fired as shown below. The velocity of the bullet is 350m/s.
Calculate the recoil velocity of the gun.

BEFORE   **AFTER**

'v'   350 m/s

2 Kg   0.01 Kg

Firing a gun is an example of an explosion where the two objects ie. the gun and the bullet, move away from each other rather than come towards each other as in a collision. As we have seen, velocity and momentum are quantities that have magnitude and <u>direction</u>. Since the gun and the bullet are moving in opposite directions we will assume that the bullet has POSITIVE VELOCITY and MOMENTUM which means that the gun has NEGATIVE VELOCITY and MOMENTUM.

Momentum before explosion = 0 !! (neither the gun nor the bullet have momentum as they are not moving)

Momentum after explosion   = Momentum of bullet + Momentum of gun

> **Remember!**
> The gun has
> **NEGATIVE VELOCITY**

$$= 0.01\text{kg} \times 350\text{m/s} + 2\text{kg} \times \text{'-v'm/s}$$
$$= 3.5 - 2v$$

Since momentum is conserved...

$$\text{TOTAL MOMENTUM BEFORE} = \text{TOTAL MOMENTUM AFTER}$$
$$0 = 3.5 - 2v$$
$$2v = 3.5$$
$$\therefore v = \frac{3.5}{2} = 1.75\text{m/s}$$

Recoil velocity of the gun is 1.75m/s.

Energy Loss During A Collision

When two objects collide momentum is always conserved. In nearly all collisions, however, the total KINETIC ENERGY AFTER the collision is LESS THAN the total KINETIC ENERGY BEFORE the collision. Energy is still conserved except that some of the kinetic energy is converted into other forms of energy eg. sound, heat, during the collision.

Kinetic energy is a quantity that has magnitude only and, unlike momentum, the direction of movement of the object is not a factor that has to be considered. You should remember from your previous studies that the kinetic energy of an object is given by the formula:

$$\text{KINETIC ENERGY (J)} = \tfrac{1}{2} \times \text{MASS (kg)} \times \text{(SPEED)}^2 \text{(m/s)}^2$$

EXAMPLE 1

Two dodgem cars are travelling in the same direction as shown below. Car A collides with car B.
Calculate the loss in kinetic energy during the collision.

BEFORE — A: 5m/s, 300kg; B: 3m/s, 200kg   AFTER — A: 4m/s, 300kg; B: 4.5m/s, 200kg

K.E before collision = KE of A + KE of B
= $\tfrac{1}{2} \times 300 \times 5^2 + \tfrac{1}{2} \times 200 \times 3^2$ = 3,750J + 900J = 4,650J

K.E after collision = KE of A + KE of B
= $\tfrac{1}{2} \times 300 \times 4^2 + \tfrac{1}{2} \times 200 \times 4.5^2$ = 2,400J + 2,025J = 4,425J

Loss in kinetic energy = 4,650J - 4,425J = 225J

EXAMPLE 2

Two dodgem cars are travelling in opposite directions. They collide and stick together as shown in the diagram.
Calculate the loss in kinetic energy during the collision.

BEFORE

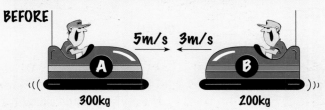

A: 5m/s, 300kg; B: 3m/s, 200kg

AFTER

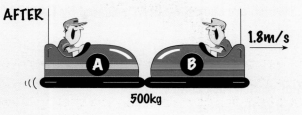

A B: 1.8m/s, 500kg

K.E before collision = KE of A + KE of B
= $\tfrac{1}{2} \times 300 \times 5^2 + \tfrac{1}{2} \times 200 \times 3^2$
= 3,750J + 900J
= 4,650J

Remember! The direction of movement of an object is <u>not</u> a factor with kinetic energy, unlike momentum.

KE after collision = KE of A + B stuck together
= $\tfrac{1}{2} \times 500 \times 1.8^2$ = 810J

Loss in kinetic energy = 4,650J - 810J = 3,840J

Elastic Collisions

These are collisions where there is NO LOSS OF KINETIC ENERGY DURING THE COLLISION. Most collisions however are not elastic and the collision in example 2 above is certainly less elastic than the collision in example 1 as a greater proportion of kinetic energy is lost during the collision.

Although there doesn't seem to be much going on, the Earth and its crust are very dynamic. Rocks at the Earth's surface are continually being broken up, reformed and changed in an ongoing, cycle of events, known as the rock cycle. It's just that things take such a long time.

Structure Of The Earth

The Earth is nearly spherical and has a layered structure as follows ...

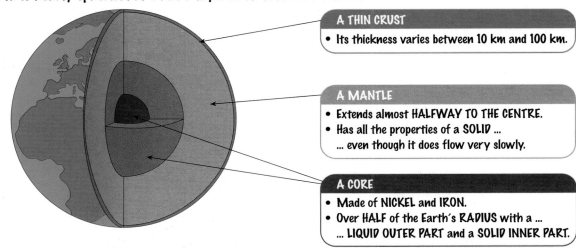

A THIN CRUST
- Its thickness varies between 10 km and 100 km.

A MANTLE
- Extends almost HALFWAY TO THE CENTRE.
- Has all the properties of a SOLID ...
  ... even though it does flow very slowly.

A CORE
- Made of NICKEL and IRON.
- Over HALF of the Earth's RADIUS with a ...
  ... LIQUID OUTER PART and a SOLID INNER PART.

- The average density of the Earth is MUCH GREATER than the average density of the rocks which form the CRUST.
- This proves that the INTERIOR OF THE EARTH is made of a DIFFERENT and DENSER MATERIAL than that of the crust.

Movement Of The Lithosphere

The Earth's LITHOSPHERE ie. the CRUST and the UPPER PART OF THE MANTLE ...
... is 'cracked' into several large pieces called TECTONIC PLATES.

These plates move slowly, at speeds of a few cm per year, ...
... driven by CONVECTION CURRENTS in the MANTLE, ...
... which are caused by HEAT released by RADIOACTIVE DECAY.

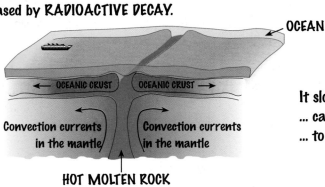

Hot molten rock comes ...
.. up to the surface ...
... at the boundary ...
... between the plates.

It slowly spreads sideways ...
... causing the plates ...
... to gradually move apart.

HOT MOLTEN ROCK

In Other Words:
New crust is formed where the rising convection current reaches the surface ...
...and old crust disappears where the convection current starts to fall.
This causes the land masses on these plates to move slowly across the globe.

EARTHQUAKES and VOLCANIC ERUPTIONS are common occurrences ...
... at the boundary between two plates.
As yet, scientists cannot predict when these events will occur, ...
... due to the difficulty in taking appropriate measurements, ...
... but at least they do know where these events are likely to occur.

The Evidence

At one time people used to believe that the features of the Earth's surface were caused by SHRINKAGE when the Earth cooled, following its formation.

Today, this is rejected in favour of the TECTONIC THEORY ...

Evidence has been gained by comparing the EAST COAST of SOUTH AMERICA and the WEST COAST of AFRICA. Although separated by thousands of kilometres of ocean, they have ...

1 <u>**Closely Matching Shapes**</u>

Geologists have long noticed that their coastlines are closely matched and were, therefore, once joined together.

HOW SOUTH AMERICA
AND AFRICA NOW LOOK

IS THIS HOW SOUTH AMERICA
AND AFRICA ONCE LOOKED?

2 <u>**Similar Patterns Of Rocks And Fossils**</u>

The East coast of South America and the West coast of Africa have similar patterns of rocks and contain fossils of the same plants and animals eg. the MESOSAURUS.

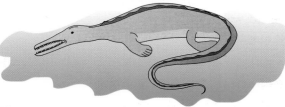

The Theory

The evidence above led Alfred Wegener to propose that ...

... MOVEMENT OF THE CRUST or CONTINENTAL DRIFT was responsible for their separation ...

... and indeed that they had at one time both been part of a single land mass.

Unfortunately Wegener was unable to explain how the crust moved ...

... and it took more than 50 years for scientists to realise ...

... that the enormous heat released during radioactive decay inside the Earth ...

... generates convection currents in the mantle, causing movement of the crust.

There is now hard evidence to show that the sea floor is spreading outwards ...

... from the junction between some plates.

We now favour his TECTONIC THEORY which explains ...

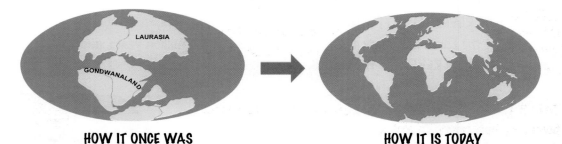

HOW IT ONCE WAS

HOW IT IS TODAY

... the movement of the continents from how they were (as GONDWANALAND and LAURASIA) to what they look like today.

Three Things That Can Happen

Tectonic plates can basically only do THREE things:

❶ Slide Past Each Other

When plates SLIDE, HUGE STRESSES AND STRAINS build up in the crust ...
... which eventually have to be RELEASED in order for MOVEMENT to occur.
This 'release' of energy results in an EARTHQUAKE.
A classic example of this is the West Coast of North America (esp. California).

❷ Move Away From Each Other – Constructive Plate Margins

When plates MOVE AWAY FROM EACH OTHER, at an oceanic ridge, FRACTURES OCCUR, ...
... these are filled by MAGMA to produce NEW BASALTIC OCEAN CRUST, ...
... at a rate of 2cm per year.
This is known as SEA FLOOR SPREADING.

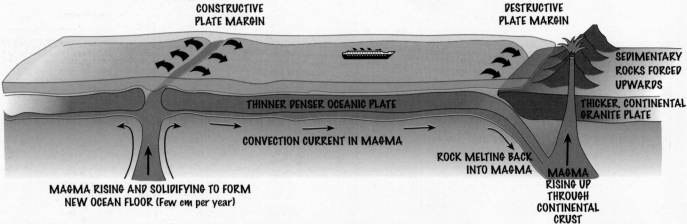

CONSTRUCTIVE PLATE MARGIN

DESTRUCTIVE PLATE MARGIN

SEDIMENTARY ROCKS FORCED UPWARDS

THICKER, CONTINENTAL GRANITE PLATE

THINNER DENSER OCEANIC PLATE

CONVECTION CURRENT IN MAGMA

ROCK MELTING BACK INTO MAGMA

MAGMA RISING UP THROUGH CONTINENTAL CRUST

MAGMA RISING AND SOLIDIFYING TO FORM NEW OCEAN FLOOR (Few cm per year)

❸ Move Towards Each Other – Destructive Plate Margins

As plates are moving away from each other in some places ...
... it follows that they must be MOVING TOWARDS EACH OTHER in other places.
This always results in the THINNER, DENSER, OCEANIC PLATE being FORCED DOWN (SUBDUCTED) beneath ...
... the THICKER CONTINENTAL GRANITE PLATE, where it partially MELTS.
This subduction forces continental crust to be compressed resulting in folding and metamorphism.
EARTHQUAKES are common and even VOLCANOES are formed ...
... due to magma rising up through the continental crust eg. West Coast of South America (Andes).

Evidence for Sea Floor Spreading

As magma rises and solidifies, to form new basaltic ocean crust, ...
... IRON-RICH minerals ORIENTATE themselves in the DIRECTION OF THE EARTH'S MAGNETIC FIELD, ...
... forming MAGNETIC REVERSAL PATTERNS parallel to the OCEANIC RIDGE.
The magnetic field of the Earth has changed NINE times in the last 3.6 million years, and ...
... this is 'mirrored' in these REVERSAL PATTERNS.

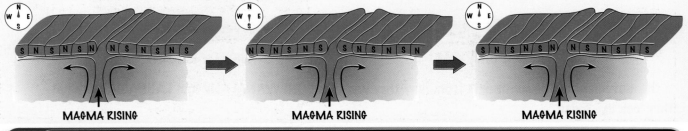

MAGMA RISING

MAGMA RISING

MAGMA RISING

TURNING EFFECT OF FORCES, MOMENTS AND STABILITY

MOMENTS

MOMENT (Nm) = FORCE (N) x PERPENDICULAR DISTANCE BETWEEN LINE OF ACTION AND PIVOT (m)

There are two ways of increasing the moment or turning force ...
❶ INCREASE THE FORCE APPLIED.
❷ INCREASE THE PERPENDICULAR DISTANCE BETWEEN THE LINE OF ACTION OF THE FORCE AND THE PIVOT.

CENTRE OF MASS

The centre of mass of an object is the point through which the whole weight, W, of the object acts.

CENTRE OF MASS

• A suspended object always comes to rest with its centre of mass situated somewhere directly below the point of suspension. This fact can be used to find the centre of mass of a thin sheet.

LAW OF MOMENTS

When an object is not turning or balanced ...

ANTICLOCKWISE   CLOCKWISE
d_2 d_1
F_2 PIVOT   C of M F_1

TOTAL CLOCKWISE MOMENTS = TOTAL ANTICLOCKWISE MOMENTS
ie. $F_1 \times d_1 = F_2 \times d_2$

STABILITY

An object will topple over if the line of action of its weight lies outside its base. When this happens the weight of the object causes a turning effect and the object will tend to fall over. The stability of the car can be increased by having a car with ...
... A LOWER CENTRE OF MASS   ... A WIDER WHEEL BASE.

C of M
W
BASE

MOTION IN A CIRCLE

The Moon and artificial satellites in orbit around the Earth, the Earth and other planets in orbit around the Sun, electrons in orbit around a nucleus and a rubber ball attached to a piece of string being whirled in a horizontal circle are all examples of objects that travel in circular (or near circular) paths.

CENTRIPETAL FORCE

The velocity of an object is its speed in a given direction. An object travelling in a circular path is constantly changing its direction and so its velocity is constantly changing. A force called the CENTRIPETAL FORCE, which acts towards the centre of the circle, is needed to produce this constant change in velocity. The centripetal force needed to keep an object moving in a circular path can vary in the following ways ...

❶ THE GREATER THE MASS OF THE OBJECT ...   ❷ THE GREATER THE SPEED OF THE OBJECT ...   ❸ THE SMALLER THE RADIUS OF THE CIRCLE ...

... THE GREATER THE CENTRIPETAL FORCE   ... THE GREATER THE CENTRIPETAL FORCE   ... THE GREATER THE CENTRIPETAL FORCE

FORCES AT A DISTANCE

The MOON and ARTIFICIAL SATELLITES are kept in their orbit by the GRAVITATIONAL FORCE OF THE EARTH.

ARTIFICIAL SATELLITE   EARTH
MOON

The EARTH and OTHER PLANETS are kept in their orbit by the GRAVITATIONAL FORCE OF THE SUN.

MARS   VENUS
MERCURY   SUN   EARTH

ELECTRONS are kept in their orbit by the ELECTROSTATIC FORCE OF THE NUCLEUS.

ELECTRONS   NUCLEUS

For an artificial satellite to stay in orbit at a particular distance, it must orbit at a particular speed to balance the gravitational force of the Earth.

MOMENTUM AND CHANGE IN MOMENTUM

MOMENTUM

The MOMENTUM of an object depends on two things ...
• THE MASS OF THE OBJECT • THE VELOCITY OF THE OBJECT
Momentum is a quantity that has both MAGNITUDE (size) and DIRECTION.

MOMENTUM (kg m/s) = MASS (kg) x VELOCITY (m/s)

p
m x v

Example ...
A car has a mass of 1,200kg. It is travelling at a velocity of 30m/s. Calculate its momentum.
Using the formula: MOMENTUM = MASS x VELOCITY
= 1,200 x 30m/s = 36,000kg m/s

VELOCITY AND MOMENTUM

If car A, below, which is moving from left to right has a POSITIVE VELOCITY and consequently a POSITIVE MOMENTUM, then car B will have a NEGATIVE VELOCITY and NEGATIVE MOMENTUM because it is moving in the opposite direction to car A ie. from right to left.

A   +ve velocity   +ve momentum   -ve velocity   -ve momentum   B

FORCE AND CHANGE IN MOMENTUM

• When two objects collide each exerts a force on the other one which is equal in size and opposite in direction resulting in each object suffering a change in momentum which is also equal in size, but opposite in direction.

• The same occurs when a force acts on a moving object: the object will experience a change of momentum for as long as the force is acting.

Δ(mv)
F x t

FORCE (N) = CHANGE IN MOMENTUM (kg m/s) / TIME (s)

One way of increasing the change in momentum without increasing the force applied is to 'follow through'. Doing this increases the time for which the force is applied.

CONSERVATION OF MOMENTUM/COLLISIONS AND ENERGY

COLLISIONS AND EXPLOSIONS

In any collision (or explosion), the momentum after the event in a particular direction is the same as the momentum in that direction before the event, PROVIDED THAT NO EXTERNAL FORCES ACT. We say that MOMENTUM IS CONSERVED.

Example ...
Two cars are travelling in the same direction along a road. Car A collides with car B and they stick together. Calculate their velocity after the collision.

BEFORE   AFTER
A 20m/s   B 9m/s   v m/s
1,200 Kg   1,000 Kg   2,200 Kg

Momentum before collision = Momentum of A + Momentum of B
= 1,200kg x 20m/s + 1,000kg x 9m/s
= 24,000 m/s + 9,000kg m/s = 33,000kg m/s
Momentum after the collision = Momentum of A + B stuck together
= 2,200kg x v m/s = 2,200v
Since momentum is conserved ...
TOTAL MOMENTUM BEFORE = TOTAL MOMENTUM AFTER
33,000 = 2,200v
∴ v = 33,000 / 2,200 = 15m/s

ENERGY LOSS DURING A COLLISION

When two objects collide momentum is always conserved. In nearly all collisions, however, the total KINETIC ENERGY AFTER the collision is LESS THAN the total KINETIC ENERGY BEFORE the collision. Energy is still conserved except that some of the kinetic energy is converted into other forms of energy eg. sound, heat, during the collision.

ELASTIC COLLISIONS ... are those where there is no loss of KINETIC ENERGY DURING THE COLLISION. Most collisions are not elastic.

EARTH STRUCTURE AND TECTONIC THEORY

STRUCTURE OF THE EARTH

• The average density of the Earth is much denser than the average density of the crust.
• Therefore the interior of the Earth must be made of a different and denser material.

THIN CRUST
MANTLE can flow slowly
CORE nickel and iron

TECTONIC PLATES ... formed in the lithosphere (crust and upper part of the mantle), move slowly due to convection currents in the mantle caused by heat from radioactive decay.
New crust is formed by the rising convection current and old crust disappears where the current falls. Earthquakes and volcanoes often occur at the boundary of the plates.

TECTONIC THEORY

Evidence for tectonic theory is based on ...
(a) Closely matching shapes of South America and Africa.
(b) Similar patterns of rocks and fossils near the coasts of the two continents.
(c) The sea floor is spreading outwards from the junction between some plates.
Wegener's theory was only accepted 50 years after it was proposed.

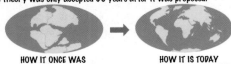

HOW IT ONCE WAS   HOW IT IS TODAY

EFFECTS OF TECTONIC ACTIVITY

THE EFFECTS ... tectonic plates can ...

(a) Slide past each other causing EARTHQUAKES eg. coast of California.

(b) Move away from each other - constructive plate margins. The fractures are filled by magma producing new basaltic ocean crust along the oceanic ridges. This is SEA FLOOR SPREADING.

(c) Move towards each other - destructive plate margins. The thinner, denser oceanic plate is SUBDUCTED beneath the thicker continental granite plate into the magma. Mountains and volcanoes may be formed here and folding and metamorphism are common eg. the Andes.

EVIDENCE FOR SEA FLOOR SPREADING

As Magma rises and solidifies, to form new basaltic ocean crust, ...
... IRON-RICH minerals ORIENTATE themselves in the DIRECTION OF THE EARTH'S MAGNETIC FIELD, ...
... forming MAGNETIC REVERSAL PATTERNS parallel to the OCEANIC RIDGE.
The magnetic field of the Earth has changed NINE times in the last 3.6 million years, and ...
... this is 'mirrored' in these REVERSAL PATTERNS.

MAGMA RISING   MAGMA RISING   MAGMA RISING

1. A spanner is being used to unscrew a nut. Give two ways of increasing the moment of the spanner.
2. Copy and complete the following table.

Force	Perpendicular distance between line of action and pivot	Moment
10N	0.2m	
20N		5Nm
	80m	12Nm
1.6N		
0.5N	1200mm	0.08Nm

3. a) What is meant by centre of mass?
   b) Where would you find the centre of mass for a symmetrical object?
   c) Describe a simple experiment to find the centre of mass of a thin sheet of material.

4. a) What is the law of moments?
   b) The diagram below shows the forces acting on a balanced object. It is pivoted at its centre of mass. Calculate F_1.

   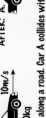

   F_1 0.3m   0.2m
   ↓F_2 = 15N   PIVOT

   c) The diagram below shows the forces acting on a balanced object. It is pivoted at its centre of mass. Calculate d_1.

   ↓F_2 = 20N d_1 0.8m
   PIVOT   ↑F_1 = 12N

   d) The diagram below shows the forces acting on a balanced object. Calculate the weight, W, of the object.

   0.4m   0.35m
   PIVOT●   ↑F = 12N
   ↓W

5. a) Why does an object topple over?
   b) The following car is on the point of toppling over. Give two ways that the stability of the car can be increased.

6. a) Give three examples of objects that travel in circular or near circular orbits.
   b) A ball attached to a piece of string is being whirled in a horizontal circle as shown in the diagram.

   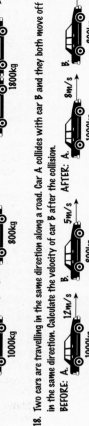

   i) What is the name of the force that acts towards the centre of the circle?
   ii) Why does a force act towards the centre of the circle?
   iii) What would happen to this force if the speed of rotation of the ball is decreased?

7. a) What force keeps the Earth in orbit around the Sun?
   b) What force keeps electrons in orbit around a nucleus?
   c) Why do artificial satellites orbit the Earth at a particular speed?

8. Does a stationary car have momentum? Explain your answer.

9. a) Calculate the momentum of a car of mass 900kg travelling at a velocity of 20m/s.
   b) Calculate the momentum of an athlete of mass 80kg who is running at a velocity of 8m/s.
   c) Calculate the momentum of a toy car of mass 800g travelling at a speed of 0.4m/s.

10. A moving truck of mass 3000kg has the same momentum as a moving car of mass 1000kg. What is the relationship between the speed of the truck and the speed of the car?

11. A truck is moving with a velocity of 18m/s. Calculate its mass if it has a momentum of 81,000kg m/s.

12. A car of mass 1200kg is travelling at a velocity of 15m/s. What happens to its velocity and its momentum if the car then travels in the opposite direction with a speed of 15m/s?

13. An object will experience a change of momentum when a force acts on it. On what two factors does this change in momentum depend?

14. a) A boy kicks a stationary ball with a force of 50N which acts on the ball for a time of 0.1s. If the mass of the ball is 0.3kg, calculate …
    i) the change in momentum of the ball.
    ii) the increase in velocity of the ball.
    b) How could the boy double the velocity of the ball without increasing the force which acts on the ball?

15. A stationary ball of mass 250g is kicked with a force of 40N. The increase in velocity of the ball is 19.2m/s. For how long was the force acting on the ball?

16. Two cars are travelling in the same direction along a road. Car A collides with car B and they stick together. Calculate their velocity after the collision.

   BEFORE: A.   12m/s   B.   10m/s   AFTER: A.   B.
   1000kg   1200kg   1000kg   1200kg →v

17. Two cars are travelling in the same direction along a road. Car A collides with car B and they stick together. Calculate their velocity after the collision.

   BEFORE: A.   12m/s   B.   5m/s   AFTER: A.   B.
   1000kg   800kg   1000kg   1800kg →v

18. Two cars are travelling in the same direction along a road. Car A collides with car B and they both move off in the same direction. Calculate the velocity of car B after the collision.

   BEFORE: A.   12m/s   B.   5m/s   AFTER: A.   8m/s   B.
   1000kg   800kg   1000kg   800kg →v

19. A gun is fired as below. The recoil velocity of the gun is 2m/s. Calculate the velocity of the bullet.

   BEFORE: 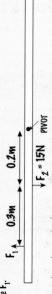 1.5kg
   AFTER: 2m/s   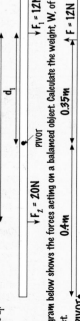   —→v 0.005kg

20. For questions 16, 17 and 18 calculate …
    a) the total kinetic energy before the collision.
    b) the total kinetic energy after the collision.
    c) the loss in kinetic energy.

21. a) What is an elastic collision?
    b) For the collisions in questions 16, 17, 18 which is the least elastic? Explain your answer.

22. a) The Earth has a layered structure. Explain what this means.
    b) What evidence is there that the interior of the Earth is made of a different and denser material than that of the crust?

23. What part do convection currents in the mantle play in the movement of tectonic plates?

24. a) What is tectonic theory?
    b) What evidence is there for the theory?

25. a) What are the consequences if two tectonic plates slide past each other?
    b) i) Explain sea floor spreading?
    ii) What evidence is there for sea floor spreading?
    c) Explain what happens when two tectonic plates move towards each other?

INDEX

All you need for the **Tested Modules ...**
... at **Double Award** and **Separate Sciences ...**

... the **Revision Guide**

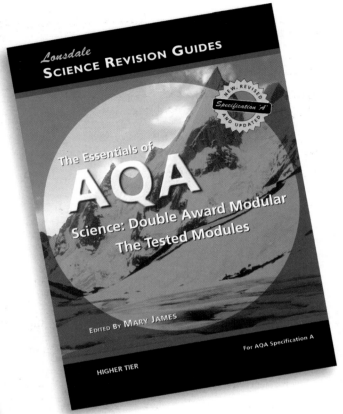

The Essentials of AQA
Science: Double Award Modular
THE TESTED MODULES

Humans As Organisms, Maintenance Of Life, Metals, Earth Materials, Energy, Electricity

- Completely updated and revised for the new AQA specification

- Contains all the relevant information and nothing more

- Also available at **FOUNDATION LEVEL**

... and the **Student Worksheets**

The Essentials of AQA
Science: Double Award Modular
STUDENT WORKSHEETS

- Completely updated and revised for the new AQA specification

- Series of student worksheets to reinforce understanding of the Tested Modules

- Every worksheet is cross-referenced to this revision guide

- Also available at **FOUNDATION LEVEL**